"In *Halfway from Home*, Montgom‹ making it clear that the two cannot rock into steadiness, ocean into exploration, grass into patience. In magnificent rhythm Montgomery patiently, steadily explores home and family. Here, place scars. Place shapes. Place rubs sometimes soft and sometimes hard. Here, Montgomery's longing for a better place burns with a kind of brilliance only someone with such profound insight can set alight."

—Nicole Walker, author of *Sustainability: A Love Story*

"Through stories personal, familial, and communal, *Halfway from Home* explores the eternal concepts of time and longing, memory and connection. In writing that is stunningly vivid, Sarah Fawn Montgomery generates an inviting and invigorating space for readers to experience her experiences, think with her through tantalizing ideas, feel nostalgia for a life that is not their own."

—Patrick Madden, author of *Disparates*

"*Halfway from Home* is like the 'treasure hole' of Sarah Fawn Montgomery's childhood—wondrous, surprising, crafted with generosity and care—a bounty born of deep excavation, as well as a deep connection with the earth itself. These essays crackle with clear-eyed insight, ache with nostalgia and grief, sing with a poet's attention to the rhythm and sound of language. When I read Montgomery's description of a wasp's nest 'swelling like a womb, like a wound above us,' I had to pause to catch my breath. Montgomery writes of rolling sentences in her mouth like bright berries; her sentences are just as brilliant and sweet and tart and nourishing for those of us lucky enough to receive them. A timely, timeless, mesmerizing collection."

—Gayle Brandeis, author of *The Art of Misdiagnosis*

"Sarah Fawn Montgomery writes with the finely moderated combination of generous vulnerability and searing intellect as she ventures with lyric intensity into the subject of climate change and its intersection with race, gender, political and social policy, and family. As an essayist, she is willing to experiment, to stretch the bounds of the form, and above all, she seeks to contextualize her experiences within the larger socio-political realities of American society. One has the alluring sense that she writes on a quest to discover, and we are grateful for her generosity in taking us along with her. *Halfway from Home* is a work of urgency, sensibility, and immediacy."

—Kwame Dawes, editor of *Prairie Schooner*

"'My earliest memory is of leaving one home in search of another,' writes Sarah Fawn Montgomery in *Halfway from Home*, a dazzling collection of essays that explores memory, nostalgia, and place; girlhood and womanhood, impermanence and time; and the question of inheritance—what we carry, the scars and secrets and stories we bear, how we leave and long for places that no longer exist, to which we can never return. Montgomery is both essayist and cartographer, charting the map of her life, measuring the distance between cities and prairies, present and past, attempting to hold on to what's been lost while looking with hope toward the future. She digs clear-eyed into the mines of her family history, excavating what's been buried and discovering what it means to be haunted. But what she finds is not all darkness. At its heart, this book is a love letter: to Montgomery's father, to her family, to the natural world; to California coastlines and the vast Great Plains, to the landscapes of one's life, to the homes we've known and the ones we're still learning to build. Montgomery has written a gorgeous, deeply felt ode to the search for belonging, to the deeply human act of seeking to find a place we might call our own."

—Melissa Faliveno, author of *Tomboyland*

HALFWAY

FROM

HOME

HALFWAY FROM HOME

ESSAYS

SARAH FAWN MONTGOMERY

SPLIT LIP
PRESS

Published by Split/Lip Press
PO Box 27656
Ralston, NE 68127
www.splitlippress.com

ISBN: 978-1-952897-25-2

Cover and Book Design: David Wojciechowski
Cover Art Elements: iStock
Editing: Lauren Westerfield

For my father—

I love you more than all the fences.

*"And even as I have been a wanderer,
all my life I have searched for home."*

—Mary Pipher

"Home is where you want to be buried."

—Kwame Dawes

EXCAVATION

Dig Site

~ San Miguel, California, 1991

What I find: a tiny wooden horse, smooth from where blade whittled wood, legs delicate as matchsticks. A golden stamp, slick replica of the ones my mother lets me lick. A tiny silver spoon with an engraving of New York State to hold in your mouth. A key to nowhere anyone knows. The rusted half of a friendship necklace—no chain. A blue button. A brassy marble. A yellow ceramic tiger.

There's a golden brooch in the shape of a turtle with emeralds for eyes, a marbled peach stone for a shell. I imagine him swimming across someone's lapel. My favorite is a tiny metal pail on its side, surrounded by spilled ceramic milk, and a Siamese kitten, head bent to lap the froth. I cup the vignette in the palm of my hand.

I find the treasure hole one Sunday, off the patio where my parents sit together watching trains clack by on the rails beyond our yard. I'm five, using a kitchen spoon to chip away at the hard dirt. At last, my father leans over to take the utensil from my hand, spooning a mound of dirt away for me, the earth softer below. He builds fences for a living and spends his days removing dirt, adding posts in such a way that erosion or strong wind won't knock them down. He knows everything about dirt, I think.

Despite the shallow divot, I find treasure, a shiny penny resting where it hadn't been before. Then a quarter, three dimes. I hold up my findings, gleeful that out of all the dirt in the backyard, I've managed to discover the sweet spot. Soon I've amassed quite a collection, an entire world in miniature, pulled from the earth with my hands.

Dig Site
~ Morro Bay, California, 1988
On hot summer days, my father drives us to the coast. He walks the length of the beach, his work boots going *squelch* in the damp, the indentations filling in with water and sand.

I struggle to leave a mark. My brief hollows fill in quickly, and no matter how far I dig my toes into the sand, as soon as I remove myself, my dents vanish as though I was never there.

Dig Site
~ Santa Barbara, California, 1975
Walking the length of a new divide, the man who will become my father uses orange paint to mark the line where he will build a fence. His work boots easily crush weeds, depress dirt. He carries a shovel shaped like an arcade machine claw, pulling up as his prize soil, rocks, and bits of vegetation, roots dangling down like worms. Over and over, he pulls earth from the same hole until a cylinder stretches several feet down, the surrounding soil like a layered cake.

He moves down the line, leaving precise holes behind. Later he fills each hole with cement, a fence post planted as if a flag. At first the flags are of discovery, of ownership, but when he builds the fence, the flags become boundaries and borders, keeping things in and out, determining where one thing ends and another begins.

Using his tools to excavate and alter the earth makes my father mapmaker, enforcer, creator. Because he shapes the soil, he shapes the world.

Dig Site
~San Miguel, California, 1993
The frog is dead, crushed beneath the foot of a boy at school and tossed into the garbage can. Patting my back as I sob, my teacher locates a small cardboard box for me to transport the creature and sends an apologetic note home to my parents.

Bumpy, I name the frog on the school bus, weeping mournfully into my father's shoulder when he comes home from work, comforted by the smell of sawdust mixed with his sweat.

Though he dutifully digs a hole, builds a cross out of wood and carves Bumpy's name, my father cannot understand why I am so comforted by the act of burial. He tells me the frog does not need such elaborate mourning when I visit the grave each afternoon, fascinated by the raised dome of dirt, sad when the sand begins to settle.

Still, he buries the next few pets, a tiny cemetery growing in the corner of our yard.

Dig Site
~ Lake Cachuma, California, 1996
At camp, we eat pudding cups in a cross-legged circle. We learn the California soil is full of Indigenous artifacts and we spend an afternoon digging and looking for shiny beads and polished arrowheads. There are enough treasures in the small plot of dirt for every child and dozens more, and we hold our beads of blue and our glinting obsidian tight in our hands as we leave the camp, head back to school past the new construction site where the first Walmart in a hundred miles is under construction.

Soon, workers discover relics and bones, and though we have learned to hold artifacts tight, a great local fight breaks out between historians and activists, city planners and bargain-minded citizens. They debate about land ownership and burial, how long ago constitutes history and where progress should begin, and they decide artifacts and the bones of the dead don't matter as much as development, and they pave right over the richness of that place, an endless parking lot for the new store at the surface.

Dig Site
~Grand Canyon, Arizona, 2008
The canyon mirrors the void in my father. After nearly thirty years with the same construction company, he is forced into early retirement. Now, without his work, he feels purposeless.

At home, he shuffles from room to room, his hands worrying at his sides. Restless.

He says little as we stand at the lip of the earth before it plunges sharp and rocky into the deep crevasse.

My mother worries he will kill himself without the joy of getting his hands dirty.

My father and I stand together in silence, unsure of who he is without his work, what we will talk about now. We are surrounded by red striation and deep purple shadow. It is hot enough to see things that aren't there.

For a long while we stare at what happens when something is carved away, disappearing with the force of time.

Dig Site
~ Mission San Miguel, California, 2012
They want the bones. At school my brothers learn about the historic Spanish mission a block from our home, the buried dead stretching beyond the low adobe walls that contain the mission graveyard, hidden for miles despite the fence. My brothers want to know why we walk on the dead, why the border hasn't been moved, why it appears one way on the surface but is so different beneath.

There is an empty lot behind the mission, a field of dirt clods and weeds, yellow mustard plant dotting the summer. My brothers use sticks and sharp rocks to dig. They are desperate to get underground.

What they find: cigarettes, old bottle caps, a rubber band so brittle from the sun it breaks at their touch, a dozen bullet casings. When we head home, their pockets jingle.

Dig Site
~ San Diego, California, 2009
My father searches for his dead brother. He drives five hours to his childhood hometown near the Mexico border, wandering the cemetery hills in his work boots and failing to locate the grave where his infant brother was buried fifty years ago. When darkness arrives, he leaves, shaking his head.

The cemetery mails a map of the grave's location and my father carries it in his pocket for weeks, folded precisely, the symmetry of his imposed order, a reminder that humans seek to shape the earth in life and death.

My family arrives at the cemetery for another exploration, and the funeral home manager leads my father to where the grave should be, taking the map, soft and faded from being opened and closed so many times, from his callused hands. She radios the office and someone brings a new map. Everyone stands, rubbing the backs of their heads in confusion

Suddenly, my father bends low to the ground, pulls out his pocket knife and plunges it into the grass. He saws at the soil.

A maintenance crew appears on a golf cart, hopping out with shovels and trowels, prepared to dig up the entire hillside. They shout from forty feet away. My uncle's casket has sunk, slipped well beyond its designated space. Ownership only extends so far down. There is his tombstone, newly excavated.

My father stares into the hole as though he is looking into his own grave.

Dig Site
~ Templeton, California, 1995, Revisited 2015
We bury the things we believe will define us after death. We bury ourselves for the future. In this way, we write the histories that will prevail.

As elementary students—the first, in fact, at this newly-constructed school—we discuss what to add to the capsule during the principal's morning announcements, during math, on the bus. We have recently discovered the radio, so we want to include music in the capsule, a Walkman if someone can manage to steal one from an older sibling. We suck sour candies each lunch period, trying to fight the grimace, so naturally, these should be included, along with Pringles and Gatorade. We want to add troll dolls, skateboards, Gak.

For weeks leading up to the burial, we debate, but it turns out the capsule is small so we have to be selective, just one item per grade. But nothing we suggest is selected, and we aren't allowed to witness the burial because administrators worry we'll dig it up and share the spoils. We never bother—none of the treasures we wanted to share with the future made it into the capsule.

It turns out the future only means twenty years, and the elementary school hopes to celebrate its anniversary by digging up what they'd buried not so very long ago. But rules at the surface are not the same. When the time comes, they cannot locate the time capsule.

Futile digging leaves the campus blemished. Eventually, people bring out metal detectors and witching sticks in their attempt to divine the past.

We lost ourselves, our best intentions swallowed up underground. Perhaps it is best we never found the parts of ourselves we buried—they never seemed accurate anyway.

Dig Site
~ Paso Robles, California, 2003
The house rumbles, guttural, like digestion. At first I think it is my younger siblings upstairs, but the vibration, I soon realize, comes from underground.

At the surface, sound becomes movement, the ground rolling underfoot, the whole world shuddering. Pictures fly off the walls, plates burst from kitchen cabinets to shatter on the floor, books slip from their shelves like the world is melting, the walls strangely liquid as the house shimmies on its foundation.

When I find my motionless siblings, wide-eyed and crying, I press our bodies together. It seems like the earth has betrayed us. We are usually unaware of its silent movement, but now the whole world is in flux and nowhere is safe.

After the shaking stops, it starts again, and again, fifty aftershocks in a few hours, magnitudes enough to make you stumble, lose balance, fall to your knees. We are on our knees all afternoon and well into the evening.

Down the street, the California mission which has stood hundreds of years splits in two, a great gash like a wailing mouth through the chapel. Gas and water lines are destroyed, so we aren't supposed to drink the water. We eat food from the fridge before it spoils and when the sun goes down, we light candles that cast shadows about the room. It looks like the walls are moving again.

The 6.6 magnitude earthquake originates in the ocean but stretches inland, leaving great cracks in the freeway like the earth is divided. I come to refer to the two sides of that highway as *before* and *after*. As then and now. What was and what will be.

The damage is worse further from the epicenter, destruction moving outwards in great circles. Brick buildings crumble in on themselves and two women are crushed to death while they shop at a local jeweler. It takes days to dig their bodies from the dust and diamonds.

An underground hot springs bursts, spewing gas and scalding water thirty feet into the air at 1,300 gallons a minute. The whole city smells of sulfur, chemical and rancid, like a burst bomb. It is difficult to see through the dust and steam.

A sinkhole forms in the parking lot of City Hall, like the earth has simply opened up and swallowed the world, dragging any semblance of order, into its stinking belly.

My father is called to build a fence around the crater.

Dig Site
~ San Miguel, California, 1995
My sandbox sits at the far corner of the yard, separated from the grass by a border of wood. I dig down along the wood to follow its edges, surprised by how quickly they end, amazed the sand and sod cooperate with such shallow order. Other times I dig deep trenches and fill them with water, smoothing the mud across my body. The mud is cool despite the summer heat and it hardens like a second skin. I can see my hairs and pores underneath, as though I am made of dirt. When I breathe, my tummy lifts like the earth is breathing with me.

I make an oven in the corner of the sandbox, using mud and patience. Each day I add another layer to what has hardened the day before. I shape the rounded dome until it resembles the adobe oven at the mission down the road. I carve an opening to serve as the oven's mouth. When the oven is complete, I bake mud pies and mud baked potatoes.

One day my father brings me a gift: a miniature set of post hole diggers, like the big ones he uses each day at work. I am ecstatic. I spend the afternoon digging in my sandbox, my hands soon covered in blisters that burst wet on the wooden handles, callusing like my father's.

I spend an entire summer digging until part of the grass caves in. Because I've been digging along the wooden border, trying to get beyond its imposed order, I've weakened the lawn. I've removed so much soil in my attempts to get underground that there is nothing left to stand on.

Dig Site
~Morro Bay, California, 2019

We squat in the sand, dipping our hands in the waves lapping at our feet. It is winter in California so my father and I wear boots to the beach, wrapping ourselves up against the cold. Though his balance is weakening, he holds his hand out to me as I struggle to walk along the slippery rocks, making my way to the tidepools.

I am visiting from Massachusetts, where I live now, far away from my father, who ages more each time I return. He still wears work boots and digs holes in the yard with his grandchildren, who know him as soft and yielding.

We peer in the tidepools, looking for guppies and anemones. Looking for our own reflections.

I have returned because the Massachusetts winters make me so lonely I could split, make me hollow and joyless, sick for my father, aging so many miles away without me. My mind is a time capsule where he is always strong, always smelling of sawdust and sweat.

I have also returned because my father is lonely in a way I have never seen. Many of his friends have died in the past few years, one hit by a car as he crossed the street, one slipping into a coma alone in his house, one shrinking with cancer until he simply disappeared. His father has died, his brothers and a grandchild sick with cancer, the earth, too, we are told, sick with fever, warming past the point of return.

My father collects his own treasures—a photo, a rock, a key—each time he loses someone, to add to a makeshift altar in his workshop.

We don't say much as we drive up and down the California coast. Nothing looks the same since my childhood, but my father knows each road and ocean inlet, like this hidden cove where the tide collects brightly colored starfish.

We sit, side by side and silent, in the watching the waves return and retreat, in the darkest part of the year, when everything seems dying and dead. We reach our hands into the holes to see what we can find.

Later, as we walk back to the car, my father stoops to gather smooth pebbles, a feather, sand dollars.

Dig Site
~ San Miguel, California, 2015

As an adult, I still have the tiny silver spoon, the small ceramic cat on the pool of milk, the golden stamp I found in the yard as a child.

During a visit home, I reflect aloud on the magic of that land. "What do you mean?" my father asks. He laughs and says he was responsible for those treasures. He says it like I've always known. When I protest, he explains.

"I dropped them in when you weren't looking."

He paints the picture of my discovery: a penny glints beneath the dirt and I use my spoon to pull it from the earth, holding it up for my father to inspect, following his suggestion to show my mother across the patio, answering her many questions about how I found it, where I thought it came from, her reminder that we lived on the California mission trail, rich with treasures. "I'd drop the next thing in while you were distracted," my father laughs, "and put a little dirt over the top."

"The hole was never more than a few inches deep."

I do not believe him. In my memory the hole was large enough for me to hide in, to fall into headfirst if I wasn't careful, the result of hours of work, of believing, of good fortune. Now that I know the truth, it seems unlikely the treasure hole's abundance could have lasted as long as it did in my mind, as it does in my memories. It must have been a few brief months of discovery before the hole was forgotten. I ask my father about time, how it must have moved in those days.

"No, you dug in that same hole for years. From age five to eight, maybe longer," my father says, and my heart lurches into my stomach. At first I think I am sad because I have been fooled for so long, but I realize that I am mourning what I thought I had—discovery, the ability to reach into the earth as far as my arm could go and grasp.

The richness of what I found! Where had my father managed to collect such things? It is this question that leaves me convinced he could not have been responsible. I list off each item, swear I've logged each excavation in my mind despite the many years between then and now. My father laughs because that I remember so well, the lines around his eyes crinkling.

"I found them on job sites," he explains. And I picture him in work boots heavy with mud and cement, wandering through fields, using his hands and his tools to lift great heaps of soil, to shape the land with his body.

Despite the noise from the tractors and the weight of the fence posts he hoists onto his back, he sees something in the dirt. He stops, bends, reaches down to sift through the soil, his fingers closing around a rock, a marble, a button, a yellow ceramic tiger. He wipes them each on his pants, takes stock of his finds, smiles at what the earth provides.

Later, he lets me do the same.

IN SEARCH OF NOSTALGIA

In the shaded grove, temperatures swell to seventy, warm enough that in winter we peel layers from our bodies like the bright-bellied lizards darting like shadows beneath our feet. We crouch beneath branches, make walking sticks of the broken bits, leaving our soft prints on the moss-laden path.

We don't need to go far to find no one—solitude and space are easy to come by in our one-stoplight town where most roads are dirt but the zip code is so expensive the place remains small despite 90s California sprawl. Our town has the best hospital for a hundred miles, and a hundred vineyards too. There is one gas station for Pepsi, another for Coke.

Drive a mile in any direction from our high school and the rolling hills embrace you. Valley oak and interior live oak compete for space with the gray pine and manzanita. Their towering branches are the only skyscrapers we rural kids have ever known.

We know nothing of cities and nature's scarcity because all the roads in and out of town lead to the beach, and in summer we pluck poppies, clutching sunshine in our hands. This is why we do not fear poison oak slinking up the trees of our Eden, though it leaves more than one of us welted and red, pus-sticky and miserable. It is easy to forget the fear of what might be when hummingbird sage blooms pink, when blue lupine and yellow mustard dot the hills, when we go to the beach to line our pockets with sand dollars.

Each day after school we pile into one another's cars and drive a mile or so until the road looks right. We park and leave the doors unlocked because around here, most everyone has what they need or want, and we walk into a field over a fence slung low like our jeans. Yes, we kick at the dandelions, but that is only because we are wishing for college or a tank full of gas to drive out to the beach dunes, where we love how the earth gives way beneath us because we aren't afraid yet to fall.

We find a spot and sit in a circle under the trees, counting down until the last time we'll be like this. We gather every day after school to play a card game called Magic and maybe it is the way the creek sounds like laughing which makes us feel like crying, or maybe it is because the sun has always made us feel like we can't sit still, like if we don't move we'll burst, or maybe it is because everything hurts so good at this age, in this place, and we want to linger a little longer.

Graduation is coming. Soon we'll scatter, moving to places where we can't park—or at least not for free. Where we won't be able to look up and see moss drip from the trees, where we won't be able to drive out to the eucalyptus grove in winter and see ten thousand monarchs nestling for warmth, the whole forest rustling and alive. We'll spread out from the coastal heart of California to bigger places like San Francisco or Los Angeles or Fresno (which we know isn't glamorous but has multiple stoplights illuminating the loneliness we'll discover).

For now, we sit in the woods imagining worlds, making magic. We survived Y2K and are trying to understand what the television says about weapons of mass destruction in a war we don't want but also don't understand, like when the guy who lost the presidential election says the climate is changing, even though here it never does, all golden warmth. Graduation looms, and with it the realities beyond our tiny town. But no one talks about that. Instead, we cling together in plain sight, storytelling between shadows and sunlight.

⬦

Even since I was a child, I've felt a sweet ache at my core, the kind of satisfaction that left me swooning, unmoored at the same time I could not fathom being more fulfilled.

I felt it while driving with my father in his beat-up pickup truck, the two of us bouncing on the stiff seats out to the dump. Every road is a backroad when you live in the middle of nowhere, and each time we approached a dip, my father pressed his foot to the pedal and down we went, slipping into the dust, my tummy somersaulting with a delightful and confusing fear.

The feeling was the same when I went camping with my parents and the trees looked familiar and foreign, making me believe I'd been there a thousand times before but also wondering if I was misremembering. Sometimes I'd see a tree in a different park or at my elementary school and my tummy would drop with remembering and I'd be happy and sad all at once. One feeling was green and another was blue, and they swirled together until I wasn't exactly sure how I felt.

When I was happy I was also sad because every good thing had to end. The smell of applesauce made me miss my grandmother even when she was in the other room, because she was aging in front of me, and the Nestle Quik she stirred up for me in tiny blue glasses was so sweet it started to sting. The tang of cranberry cookies reminded me of the first time my future sister-in-law came to visit and she was tall and pale like me but said aloud all the sharp witty things I thought but kept inside. Often, the surge would accompany memories of home—the smell of sawdust taking me back to my father's workshop, an empty pasture stretching seemingly forever, or the sun hitting the road right as an old odd song came on the radio.

When I moved away to start my life somewhere else—convinced, like many millennials, that this fresh start would mean success—I missed home all the time. When I moved to Nebraska for graduate school the sweet ache rarely came, less often still when years later I moved to Massachusetts to begin a job. I was so busy making my way in the world that I did not realize how quickly it had changed. By the time I stopped to realize, America was no longer the home nation I'd known, but instead a danger I could not fathom. A new climate and political control meant the country was now constantly on guard, our nation pulsing its many grievances. Everywhere was a throbbing hurt and I missed the homeland of my youth like I missed my actual home, neither of which existed anymore.

"The pain a sick person feels because he is not in his native land, or fears never to see it again," wrote Swiss medical student Johannes Hofer in his 1688 thesis, coining the term *nostalgia* to posit a new disease. Combining the Greek terms *nostos*, meaning "returning home," and *algia*, meaning "pain," Hofer posited a new disease whose symptoms included anxiety, insomnia, irregular heartbeat, lack of appetite, fever, pallor, and muscle weakness. While it may seem odd now to define nostalgia as pathological, up until the later part of the twentieth century it was regarded as both a medical disease and a mental illness, not merely sadness but a deep hopelessness, victims seeing ghosts, committing suicide, suffering from strange magic.

Doctors throughout the 18th and 19th centuries searched for a pathological nostalgia bone in the human body. Spanish soldiers during the Thirty Years' War were discharged due to *el mal de corazón*, or heart sickness. Germans were diagnosed with *heimweh*, or home pain. When the Russian army experienced an outbreak of nostalgia on its way to Germany in 1733, the general told troops that those with the virus would be buried alive to stop the spread, following through on his threat several times in order to protect the masses.

Swiss soldiers, often hired during the late 17th and early 18th centuries to fight in other countries' wars, were believed to be particularly affected by nostalgia. Drawn away from their homelands, the Swiss soldiers were dismissed from military service as a result of nostalgia so frequently that playing or singing particular Swiss milking songs was forbidden, punishable by death. While military doctors blamed the symptoms on ear and brain damage from Swiss cowbells, Hofer suggested Swiss mercenaries fighting in the lowlands were homesick for the Alpine landscape, feverish and fainting, sometimes so ill they succumbed to death.

Nostalgia was believed to be dangerous. Obsessing over memories of home, Hofer posited, drew spirits to certain areas of the brain, leaving gray matter elsewhere deprived until vital functions slowed and eventually ceased. The epidemic of nostalgia spread throughout Europe and North America in the 18th and 19th centuries, easily transmittable if one was isolated from home. To leave one's home under duress—be it from war, famine, plague, or the need to search for a better life—was to suffer eternally.

Contemporary research, however, suggests that nostalgia acts as neurological protection, increasing empathy and understanding, and creating meaningfulness, connectedness and continuity between the past and present. Research on nostalgia reveals a universality of the feeling across both countries and continents and demonstrates that, despite cultural differences, nostalgia creates compassion and social connectedness for many, preventing loneliness and alienation. Our universal desire for emotional equilibrium is why, despite cultural differences, we experience nostalgia more frequently in times of change or uncertainty. Why we crave its sweetness when the world stings. Nostalgia allows us to create a stable space in a world where these things are increasingly rare, where nowhere is safe and nothing is permanent.

Nearly twenty years after I left it, the town where I went to high school now boasts a handful of stoplights while my rural hometown has none. As a working-class kid whose parents could never afford my school's zip code in the wealthy town neighboring our own, I smooth-talked my way into the district, my grades boosting the school's reputation.

My hometown was miles away in a place where most everyone spoke Spanish and the smell of street tacos meant it was Sunday, folks taking to the streets after Catholic Mass at the historic mission I could see from my front yard. The train bisected my town like an artery, a good side and a bad side just like in the movies, though when my school friends and their parents found out where I lived, sides didn't seem to matter. All of my town was bad news, they said, checking to make sure their cars were locked before coming inside. This usually happened right before they stopped coming at all.

When the train rattled through my hometown—to somewhere better, somewhere most of us would never go because nearly everyone stayed put—the rails sent dust through the streets. The dust covered the rusted cars lining the sidewalks and covered the hand-lettered signs for tiny businesses too—pastelerías, tamales, alterations, and eventually my mother's home daycare. It coated our shoes with the dried-up reminder of where we came from.

The fields, too, were brittle and barren, full of rattlesnakes, lizards without their tails, and baby rabbits my old cat caught and brought, scared and still, to our doorstep where she then dismantled them, leaving their entrails and heads like offerings. Sometimes a rabbit survived and ran scared around our yard, dashing through the rose bushes my mother worked so hard to grow from nothing. The shrieking made me afraid, like the shouting and stabbings at the town's one bar where more than once, someone staggered outside and died.

It was so dry that every summer fires swept over the surrounding hills, leaving them black and smoking. We did not have a police station or sheriff but we did have a fire station, the threat of burning imminent. But when our town did catch fire, it did not make the local news; no one worried about the place I called home.

That I did not belong to the town where I went to school was clear by the way my classmates would not come to my house, or when, years later, I ran into a classmate and inquired about "our town" and she simply laughed and said, "It was never yours."

But I also did not belong to my own town. I spent most of my time away just like my parents, who both commuted to wealthy areas to work long hours. I had no neighborhood friends, so I spent my time outside with trees and rocks and bugs, daydreaming about leaving the past behind and moving somewhere better in the future.

&

We did not notice the world had changed until we were trapped inside, and now we are nostalgic for a time that will not return. The town I used to pretend was mine no longer exists. The oak trees have mostly been cut, the hills crowded with vineyards that bleed the soil dry, subdivisions slotted into precision. Fences line what used to be backroads, along with trespass warnings. The creeks we frequented as children are long dried up. Each year, fires ravage the land.

Though nostalgia stretched across cultures for hundreds of years, our sense of longing has changed. Impermanence is the only permanent quality of modern life—destruction all we seem to create—and so our etymologies and pathologies must change. First described by philosopher Glenn Albrecht in the aftermath of 9/11, *solastalgia* names the emotional and existential pain we feel in the wake of uncontrollable environmental distress. A homesickness felt even while at home, an inescapable dread that all we love will be soon be dead, our sense of safety shifting beneath our feet, burning before our very eyes. The ache is not sweet but a kind of shock, the realization that the land we stand on is under threat from earthquakes, tornados, hurricanes, drought. Flowers of our youth replaced by dusty fields; beaches closed for oil spills.

The friends I have not spoken to since high school—each of us drifting away like we knew we would when we clung so tightly to one another and made magic in the woods—raise their children in a new world. The polar caps are melting and children witness gaunt polar bears on television between commercials for the companies leading greenhouse emissions. Gone are the woods and the shaded groves, most of the monarchs, and even some of us.

I purchased my first home in late 2019, before the start of the end of the world. Within months of moving in, the world shut down and we were left to mourn what was and to fear what was coming. I ache with the nostalgia of my childhood but find that luckily—for now—my home in Massachusetts is not so different: the dirt road leads to the shore, seasons cycle in a constant thrum of ending and beginning. Nestled on a few acres isolated from others, I am still alone with the trees and rocks and bugs.

Like the woods of my childhood, here I know nothing of scarcity. I crouch beneath branches, make walking sticks of the broken bits, leave my soft prints on the moss-laden path. In summer I snap asparagus that grows wild in my yard, pluck berries from the vine. When I spy the goldenrod blooms, white yarrow and pink astilbe dotting the meadow, the sweet surge comes and I do not know if I hurt from remembering something past or from hoping this brief moment will last.

Red foxes dart about the yard, along with coyotes that wrestle on the lawn at midnight. Great blue herons swoop low through the clearing before landing to nest in the wetlands, and a red-tailed hawk preens on a perch waiting for field mice. Deer walk their fawns through the meadow to eat, and groundhogs gorge on clover. It seems like the last of the honeybees gathers at the bloom.

There is magic here, I know. I am full of missing what is right in front of me.

But I am already wanting something that isn't there. This is only home because it will be gone one day. Because I will go somewhere else, in search of nostalgia, a lifelong habit of saying goodbye.

CHRONOSTASIS

Evening ticks by, the sun retreating behind the rolling hills surrounding our small house, which means it is night. Except this answer isn't good enough for tomorrow's test.

I'm learning to tell time by memorizing placements on a clockface designed to look like the shifting shadow of a sundial. The numbers are written in cursive like a frightening premonition of what time means—looping as a noose, bleeding imperceptibly from one moment to the next.

Both hands up means midnight, which makes sense because one disappears behind the other like the moon behind a cloud. Straight up and down means halfway. But I can't keep track of the shapes that mean division, why a quarter is fifteen in time but not money, why half is thirty. Time relies on arbitrary rules, which is why the grownups like it so, tied to the clock so that a tickle fight or a hold-your-breath contest is over if the time insists.

My mother quizzes me and says I can learn time, which I believe because, already at age five, memorizing what others expect from me is easy. But Cogsworth is the worst character in *Beauty and the Beast*, telling everyone when to be, and I don't want to look at shapes and see responsibilities. Already, the sound of the clock hand lurching forward follows me like an echo, keeps me up at night even though my mother says it's not that loud and go to sleep.

Time is frustrating, always leaving before I realize. One moment I'm thinking and the next the thought is already gone, even the me in the mirror is gone. It's hard to hold onto what's here, like how a dandelion disappears before my lips form a kiss, or a chrysalis bursts open, the moth inside spreading wings to fly up and away like the summer.

I learn that time changes a person. My father is one man early in the morning before the sun comes up, the two of us hugging in front of the heater, talking about growing vegetables and how to hold a hammer, but when the clock hits 5:30 a.m. he's another, rushing to get out the door and on the road, angry, stressed, already thinking about hours ahead in his day, worrying he will be hours behind in his tasks. My grandmother is different than she was last year, before my mother's father died, a shadow crumpling in on herself more each month. And the girl I was an hour ago is different than the girl I am now. I miss myself, that girl from an hour ago. But missing yourself doesn't make sense, so I keep it inside.

I wonder if they had regrets, the ones who divided infinity and called it time.

&

When you watch the second hand on a clock freeze before lurching forward, you exist across time. In other words, time travel is possible.

For a brief second the brain cannot comprehend the construction, resists the method of organization. Time marches forward, the same monotony and rhythm, but our mind creates a false memory of the frozen hand.

Chronostasis—the illusion that chronology stretches backwards—reveals our longing for the past.

&

Tamagotchis are everywhere in middle school, cradled in our hands during math when we learn about angles and remainders, the goal to take what is whole and break it apart. The egg buzzes several times a day as a reminder that survival is not guaranteed.

We pass them around at recess like currency. We clip the Tamagotchis on our backpacks and listen to the plastic eggs click together while we walk through the halls, lockers slamming, bells sounding out the passing of each class and hour.

The game is simple: keep it alive. Except the longer it lives, the harder it is to maintain the creature's happiness. You have to feed Tamagotchis endlessly, their hunger deep and aching. You have to clean up after all their life mistakes. You have to exercise them and take them outside for fresh air when you are stuck inside in front of a board full of math problems to solve.

I am no good at keeping things alive, no good at responding to the endless buzz of the egg's timed reminders. My eyes are outside on clouds that look like trains rushing elsewhere, that undulate like the jellyfish that fascinate me at the aquarium, their bodies billowing and bursting. I'm always rolling in the grass tracing the blades with my fingertips, finding roly-polies to wander the length of my life lines. When they get to the end of my hand, the roly-polies fall, and I wonder what it's like to wander from the prescribed narrative, to plummet free from time.

I forget time at the ocean, the tides past and present at once, waves erasing their own existence, a seashell to my ear like a song. Except it's not the ocean I hear but the sound of my heartbeat, a reminder that long ago, before eons and hours, I came from the sea.

I forget when my father and I dig in my treasure hole, plucking quartz and old pennies from deep inside the earth, or when we wander through new construction, the skeletons of houses we can never afford casting shadows in the sunlight. My shadow stretches long ahead, a version of myself unafraid to slant unexpected, to claim the unknown.

I forget time when my parents whisper at night about late bills or when I try to sleep alone, afraid of fire and the ghosts that haunt our family, making them drink too much.

Tamagotchis remind me that time is a scolding. I've always missed the past or am worrying over the future. Even when I do what I'm supposed to do in the present, I have to keep doing it forever to avoid failure's looming shadow.

Time after time, I let my creature die, the little ghost of itself hovering on-screen. It's supposed to be a shame, a sign I have failed the game. But the ghost looks buoyant, boundless. It looks free.

When our teacher says it is impossible to escape time, I make the clock bleed.

I don't mean to spite her—it's just that the clock is pushing in like the walls, like how there is a right way to sit and raise your hand and read a book. Time is a rule like hurry, like sorry, like quiet.

I am exhausted by time before it has begun, am only interested if it's to think about how I am different with each grain that falls through the hourglass on the teacher's desk during timed tests, except this is not a quiz question, not on the standardized state test and no, no Sarah Fawn, no one will ask if a tree knows it's aging, knows how it rings around its previous selves, knows if the time at the surface is the same as at the root.

It's not so difficult, injuring time. Simply press your nail to the screen of an LCD clock and watch the numbers blur. Pixels shift, precise at first, sharp fractal and edge, but then pressure breaks boundaries and the shapes go soft and squiggle, like liquid, like escape.

The teacher says stop before it is too late. I say watch me split. I press harder until now becomes then.

♨

The invention of the pendulum clock in 1656 erased time.

Until then, clock accuracy averaged a deviation of fifteen minutes a day, as though it were possible to live across memory and history.

Fifteen minutes a day is a significant portion of the mayfly's 24-hour lifespan after they emerge from water nymphs to fly to the sky. Fifteen minutes a day of meditation can recircuit neural networks in the brain. Fifteen minutes of sunshine is enough to maintain the vitamin D levels that keep you happy. In 1968, Andy Warhol predicted, "In the future, everyone will be world-famous for fifteen minutes." In fifteen minutes you can walk a mile or sleep with your lover. Songs like Elton John's "Your Song," REM's "Losing My Religion," and Queen's "Crazy Little Thing Called Love" were written in fifteen minutes.

With the clock's invention, however—a swinging weight around its neck—the accuracy of clocks improved. The deviation shrunk to a mere fifteen seconds a day.

But a pendulum clock can only keep time if it is still, motionless. It can only track the movement of the world if it doesn't move at all.

In contrast, many contemporary clocks are accurate enough to keep time for twenty million years. They will not gain or lose a second. The Cryogenic Sapphire Oscillator, which ticks ten billion times per second, will keep accurate time for forty million years. The strontium clock can keep time without losing a second for some five billion years, and recent advancements on the strontium clock suggest it will now keep time for ninety billion years.

Maintained since 1947, the Doomsday Clock records scientists' predictions that the world will end in human-made global catastrophe. Humanity uses the clock to measure time in metaphor. In this way we cease to exist at all—looking to future suffering as payment for the past.

The Doomsday Clock's original 1947 setting was seven minutes to midnight—our inevitable destruction. Since then, it has been set backward and forward twenty-four times, waxing and waning like the moon. After the Cold War, scientists optimistically moved the clock seventeen minutes away from midnight in 1991. Now, however, we creep ever closer due to climate change as the clock jumped to only one hundred seconds until midnight in 2020.

Listen closely and you will hear the sound of the seconds like a terrible metronome marching you towards the inevitable. Your frantic heartbeat slows. This means time is slipping away.

◊

As a child I lie in bed, worrying about time. It is running out, which means I am already dying, am a fearful ghost haunting my own room, my chance at sleep slipping through my fingers like sand, the next day destined to be a blur, dreamlike without the watercolor and whimsy.

I do not like clocks that make sounds. Even the eyelash hand of a watch buried deep in my closet is enough to wake me. I do not like the turning gold clock on my father's desk, the way it spins like a carousel. I do not like windup clocks that require my effort and time only to tell me it has passed. I do not like the green glow of the digital clock on the wall like a wrong moon. I turn and turn, away from the sound or the glow, my body twisted as if trying to run backwards.

At sleepovers the loneliness creeps in when the lights go out and I can hear the clock over the sound of my friends breathing. I bury myself in my sleeping bag to drown out the noise but all I hear is the sound of my heartbeat, a clock I can't escape.

At recess my friends collect quarters to call POPCORN to ask the time and I think why bother because it is already gone after the receptionist delivers it, gone more by the time your ear hears, further disappeared by the time you register it, hang up the phone to tell your friends.

In science we make clocks out of potatoes and the teacher comments on how accurately we've captured time. I do not want a potato clock, do not want time to be mine, instead preferring to put a potato in water in the window and to watch it transform, vining through time, looping to infinity.

The only clock I'm intrigued by is the VCR, which keeps the now when you go back to then. I crave the ability to rewind like I do in my head at night playing over the good and bad parts of my day, favorite memories whose contours begin to blur in my mind until I doubt them altogether. I like repetition, soothed by the way it makes time disappear. I rewatch the same shows, delighted by how I know what to expect yet always looking for something new. I watch them forward, then send them back. I like the way the machine puts lines through the image, the numbers running backwards, the screeching sound it makes when the narrative will not obey the rules. I like to watch the shining ribbon reel from one side of the tape to the other, the seamless way the story can begin again.

&

In 1748, botanist Carl Linnaeus proposed a garden featuring flowers whose petals opened at particular times of day according to sunlight levels. His flower clock relied on the plants' natural circadian rhythms—those we are now warned to protect from the blue light of our screens. To tell time, Linnaeus theorized, you simply needed to look at nature.

The term "counterclockwise" was invented after the popularization of timepieces. Prior to this, the direction was referred to as "widdershins," which meant "against the course of the sun."

Deep inside an East Texas mountain rests a clock taller than the pyramids of Giza. Once a year the clock ticks. The century hand advances every hundred years. The cuckoo comes out each millennium.

Powered by the Earth's thermal cycles, the clock is free from human design, except that Amazon's Jeff Bezos is partially responsible for its expensive upkeep. The clock is symbolic, Bezos says, "An icon for long-term thinking."

Designed to withstand time itself, the clock is expected to tick uninterrupted for ten thousand years, echoing our contemporary concepts of time deep inside the belly of the earth.

We are poised to leave middle school and begin high school, poised to leave childhood and begin adulthood, recess and play vanishing like the world will, the news promises, once the new year and millennium strike.

Time exists to mark our living, to measure our survival. But scientists didn't account for the turn of the century, predictions warn. When 1999 clicks to the new millennium, timekeepers won't be able to keep up, will grind to a halt, cogs and pendulums frozen without direction.

Without our clocks, time will not exist, and without a way to mark our progress, our survival, what will become of humanity? Around the world, people stock up on food, emergency kits, water, cash. Doomsday preppers stare straight into the camera on the nightly news. Each year we turn to the clock to countdown the passing of time though nothing changes.

The warning pulses through my middle school like a vein. Teachers don't know how to downplay clocks since their lurching hands order our days. It should be fine, they promise, staring hard at the clock. When the bell rings at the hour, we all jump.

As an adult, I wake to the clock beside my bed. Walking to the kitchen, I spy my phone on the counter, flashing with reminders that have gone off in the night, though I am forever refusing notifications. There is a clock on the microwave, another on the stove, another on the television, everywhere the green glow of time.

Sometimes I put my phone on airplane mode, pretending I'm traveling, free from time for a moment or an hour. Flying is a kind of time travel, departures and arrivals before and after you've just been, as though you are living in two times, or, I prefer to think, you are living as two selves, more, existing in multiple in all the various times.

When a plane lands, people turn on their phones at once, scrambling for texts and news alerts and phone calls, the whole plane vibrating with time. I like to leave my phone off, to wonder when and sometimes who I am, and to wander disoriented through the hangar to the arrival and departure screens, surprised when I finally encounter the time, a lovely recognition. When I fly home to California from where I live in Massachusetts, crossing time zones and great distances like a space traveler, I spy Nebraska, another former home, another me in another time. No matter when I am or where I go, I am always halfway from home.

I once spent the transition to Daylight Savings Time in Arizona. I woke early each morning, my body so accustomed to waking hours earlier on the East Coast, and sat in the dark, waiting for the world to start. On this day, time shifted on each coast around me, the usual reminders ringing out on the news. But here the time did not change. I was not *before* or *after*, only unbound, unburdened.

&

Two scientists set out flying across the world with four clocks as companions.

They circle the globe fully once, going east. They fly against the sun.

When their 1971 trip is complete, they circle the globe once more, this time heading west, as if trying to outrun sunset, the day's inevitable end.

The scientists compare the clocks when they land. They look at the time they've kept in the sky against the time kept on earth and find that time has dilated. Time is only consistent on earth. Nothing is what they expect. The narratives don't match.

Time only exists if you don't fly too high, if you keep your feet rooted on the ground.

IN FLAMES

The New Year begins in flames. The final hours of 2018 are cold in New England, wind bitter with crystals of ice, frigidity leaching into bone until folks become brittle. Eve shifts to day, the dark replaced with weak winter light struggling to find its way through the fog. The world is quiet, coast to coast, sleeping away merriment or misery from the previous night, the previous year. We sleep late because we want to wake to hope instead of the same arduous winter and world.

In the pre-dawn of the new year, a woman, seventy-two, enters her car with her seventy-five-year-old friend. They bundle against the cold together, turn up the heat, hoping the vehicle and their bodies will warm quickly. She turns the key; the car lurches.

The car drives over an embankment, through the side of an apartment building, and into the basement laundry where it severs the gas lines, flames sparking in the dark.

The room burns quickly along with the bodies, black and smoking, but the flames hunger further, slurping into the hallway, scorching the walls, licking up the ceiling. Fire drips like rain. The building is old, so the alarms delay before crying out danger to residents, many of whom—including several of my friends—have just poured themselves into bed, unwilling to accept this cruel luck, believing it to be a fire drill or a mishap like burned eggs.

Flames claim the first floor, the second. They spread, greedy and indifferent.

My husband and I awake to a frantic call for help and rush to pick up the friends we toasted with hours before. The previous year had been hard, each of us struggling to adapt to our new professions in Massachusetts, as we were hopeful that what was ahead would be better than what we wanted to leave behind. But when we arrive at their apartment complex, the air is thick and noxious. We struggle to breathe and see our friends blinking bleary-eyed through the smoke in their pajamas, clutching their cats. They climb in the back of our car, and we drive silently through what looks like apocalypse.

◊

Lately I search for flames. When I moved to Massachusetts in 2017, I was unused to a sun that abandoned the sky each winter. That first season, the loss made me ache with regret, made rising from bed to make my way in the world a burden. Without the sun my new home felt friendless, even with my husband at my side, and my mind began to skid and dart, so desperate was it for light and spark. Month after month, my mind tried to create its own heat, but the only thing that burned was me, compulsion and fear swelling in the dark.

When the sun returned in May, I was a fearful wreck, so convinced that the dark meant I was dying, was dead inside already. When the world began to bloom, slowly, slowly, the ice eased from my bones. I began to thaw and I could breathe. But I still starved for heat.

Against advice, I looked up, straight into the heart of the sun, and tried to hold my gaze. I nearly cried, not from the hurt, but from the sure ache that it would leave again.

Now, each winter, I encircle myself in fire. I build a shrine. Each afternoon, as the faint light fades too soon, I ignite a dozen candles, make myself a miniature hearth. There is never enough fire.

The flames do not keep me warm, but they do surprise me. No matter how many candles I light, I cannot say which way each will go. I know that today it is dark, and tomorrow it will be dark, and that darkness is the only constant ahead. But the flames resist prediction.

◊

When California blackens with flames, I feel nothing. I do not know if this is because home is dead or because I am.

The news shows images of towns gone to rubble, eaten up by fire and spit back out. The forest is gone; smoke rises from the soil. The man who is president says the flames came because we were careless. Fire shows no kindness. Either fear it or be consumed.

From across the country, friends send me photos of inferno—sky ablaze, ravaged hillsides, ash raining down. They can't breathe, they say, are quarantined inside because the air is thick with smoke.

A friend's grandmother—from the town Paradise—is lost. She lives alone at age ninety and no one can get to her home because the road is on fire, the hill is on fire, the town, the county, the state is on fire. Flames jump highways, bleed to the ocean. Firefighters fly in from around the country. In photos, they are tiny as ants.

The family posts a photo of the frail woman on social media. "Contact if seen," they plea to everyone, to no one. In the photo, the woman stares straight into the camera. She looks as though she is hollow.

My friend rests her hand on her stomach, her first child inside. She pulses red. Each day she waits for her son to be born, for news that her grandmother has been found. Each day, instead, the news reports the latest political apocalypse, reports the California fire death toll rising. The air in Paradise must smell of burning foliage and flesh.

After a week, two, Thanksgiving draws near, and my friend admits that she is waiting for her grandmother's body. She wants the closure of bone.

My mother gives me a children's Bible when I am five. Of all the illustrations, Sodom and Gomorrah fascinates me most. In the illustration, flames lick the heels of women as they run from the burning city. The women have dark hair and eyes, long white nightgowns like the childhood ones I wear to bed, my father tucking me in each night, though I never stay in his careful cocoon for I am afraid the house will catch on fire. I see flames in my dreams and wake up coughing, gasping for breath, begging my parents to let me sleep in the safety of their room where I am not alone. I believe I am a girl destined to burn.

God scorches those who sin, my children's Bible teaches. The Bible features a world on fire. We are sinners, all of us dancing, burning.

I turn to the story of Sodom and Gomorrah frequently, for it is one that features women, and I imagine the figures come to life, memorizing the shapes of their soft bodies. I do not understand what they have done to burn. Why they must flee, skirts tangling between their legs.

One woman stands tall as the others crouch, crawl away from the flames. She is important, I know, but only because she is wicked. The book does not give her a name. I am drawn to her most, for unlike me, she is not afraid. She does not hide her face under her quilt or call to her father a dozen times a night to save her.

Instead, she turns to face the fire, turns to salt, glittering, bitter.

Throughout the summer after the fire that consumed my friends' apartment building, the fire alarms in my Massachusetts apartment sound, though there are no flames or smoke. Repair men cannot determine why the building is alarmed, why the machines sing warning. I think of my friends, their lost home. Over and over, a canary's warning chirp.

Repair men replace batteries in one smoke detector, another. They replace one machine, another. Still, my husband and I are surrounded by warnings whistling. I worry it is not the machines but the wires, that the electrical cords will snap, flames sparking in the dark. My cats do not trust the sound and scurry beneath the bed.

One night the alarm sounds like it has for so many weeks. I turn over to sleep, because I am dulled to the threat. I no longer know what to fear.

I believe the noise is the usual false alarm until I smell smoke, open the curtains from my vantage point on the top floor and witness the whole building lighting up red and white, sirens crying out, residents streaming out the door to safety.

My grandmother set the kitchen ablaze with a cigarette because she was careless. That's what the family says of the 90s fire that left the walls black and smoking, but that isn't what stained the home where my grandmother lived with my grandfather and my frightened mother while he drank and shouted.

The story goes like this: my grandmother was cooking and singing and sneaking sips of his whiskey and looking out the window to a future she would have preferred, and the cigarette fell from her fingers. Lazy, selfish, they say of women who make mistakes. Who make fire.

At least, this is the version I am told. I was only a child then. But I prefer the version where she was tired of the "Grey" patrilineal name she married, tired of walls that looked like cinderblock. I prefer the version where she wanted color, heat, wanted her body to swell rather than shrink with touch. Where she preferred a world on fire, redemption in flames. Where she did not need alarms to tell her there was danger in the house.

After the fire, she papered the walls in yellow. In the dark, they glowed.

🔥

A dozen scars line the length of an adopted brother's spine. They are symmetrical, stacked precise like each vertebra that shuffles beneath his gaunt frame. "Failure to thrive," social workers said when he moved in with my family from foster care at three.

The scars shine in the dark, reminders to the boy, now a man, of where his birth father used his infant son to extinguish cigarettes.

🔥

This winter, the start of this new decade, I build a shrine of fire to warm bone. There is never enough fire so I light candles and buy a tiny electric fireplace with flames like a child's cartoon drawing. It is a poor representation of the heat I seek. False god.

So, too, is the light I pray to each morning. In these early years back East, while I still feel frigid and alone in this landscape that does not warm or welcome me, where I feel the winters cruel and indifferent, and with them my neighbors, I purchase a light that promises to replace the sun. I sit with it and my loneliness each morning, try to convince my mind it's manageable.

Because I've walked the slick line of dread, coming threateningly close to plummet, seasonal depression leaving me feeling like I'd rather not exist, I follow this ritual, however mundane. I sit close, closer still to my fake sun each morning. My first years in Massachusetts, I am motionless, tethered to a machine. The only thing that feels real is the danger that comes from looking directly into the light.

🔥

In the weeks after my friends' home burns to the ground, another friend asks her landlord if he will provide a fire ladder for the two-story home she rents. She has seen how fire can strip a home back to bone.

No, he says, hanging up the phone. The line buzzes dead.

🔥

"Visit me. I'm so lonely."

That's what she'd said, pleaded even, the girl I'd known since elementary school, back when we were girls becoming women. When I arrived, I found her crouching, gray.

She'd lost her faith, she said, the girl I'd known since elementary school. She'd believed, run from burning cities, never turned back like the other sinners. But now she tried to find warmth in bodies, a late-night rotation that left her feeling like a fluorescent laundromat at 3:00 a.m.

That night we went to a college party, held red cups in our hands and snuck sips of warm whiskey. She drank too fast, laughed too loudly in the cinderblock garage. She moved from lap to lap and when someone handed her a cigarette, she held it to her mouth like a kiss.

We did not smell flesh—she'd forgotten to turn the cigarette around—but we heard the sizzle of flame extinguished. Afterward, her

lip bore the scar of what happens when you are so numb you don't
know you are burning.

✤

He won't say what haunts him, my other firefighter brother. When he
was fifteen, the local fire station wanted to make a space for an adopted boy who had already seen too much. They wanted him to see hope
in flames extinguished.

At first he swept the station, washed the trucks. But he was desperate and needy for affection. He hungered, seethed. One afternoon
they let him sound the alarm.

Soon he rode along to pull cats from trees, then bodies pinned between trucks and trunks. Before he had a driver's license, my brother
talked to a man while the car trapping him down combusted.

He did not say so at first, but he could not keep the secret and
cried out in his sleep, gasping for breath.

✤

I watch fire roll down the golden hills that surround our dusty California town, but I am not afraid. This happens every summer, as much
a part of the season as elementary summer school and popsicles. My
skin burns in summer and I shed like the lizards I love to catch, their
tails wriggling beneath my fingers after they escape. I do not think
them hurt; I believe them metamorphosized. Beneath my burn, I too
am transformed, the skin shining and ready.

Under the California sun, I dart in and out of the sprinklers, stopping now and then to inspect the burning hillside. The fire rolls like
the syrup from my Sunday pancakes: viscous, determined. My parents
murmur to themselves, my mother rushing in and out of the house to
make phone calls to her mother who lives nearby. I sniff the air.

Though I fear fire in the night, I love the smell of burn like I love
the smell of propane. The smell means standing with my father by
the heater at 4:30 a.m. for an hour before he leaves for work, his arms
wrapping me in safety. It means my mother baking cookies, licking
sticky sweet from my fingertips. Our propane tank stands in the front

yard, a white potbellied behemoth I pat like a cow when I walk by. My cow must be hot, I realize, lifting the sprinkler to hose her down.

My parents and I survey the fire creeping closer to our home, waiting to see when we should flee. My parents say they hope the fire does not jump the freeway.

This is the first time I realize flames are alive.

❧

Notre Dame is burning. I watch on television—like I've watched much of 2019—gape-mouthed. Angels weep and gargoyles crouch as if to pounce on the citizens gathered below. The archway doors are etched with the last judgment; the inferno is in the house. One side depicts those who will ascend, rise from ash triumphant. On the other, those who will forever burn.

I am a professor, and as students shuffle from class to class, I wonder if they are afraid. They have grown up with apocalypse, school shootings and environmental decay, a world obsessed with its end, one where there is no one to pull us headlong from danger, deliver us into safety.

In-between coverage, the screen goes black. I see my reflection in the empty screen. But I do not jump when the spire falls.

❧

In summer the sun has fully returned, and slowly, slowly the warmth. My friends have found a new home, begun to replace their lives. My other friend misses her lost grandmother but has delivered a new son who is bright-eyed like a bird. The alarms in my building are silent at last and my husband and I drive around searching for our first home to purchase.

When my friends and I gather for a BBQ, I breathe in the smell of propane and flames and think of California. I think of my childhood summers, how much I miss them now that they are gone. I think of my parents promising to protect me from the danger, how much I believed they could, there in the golden light.

I remember, too, how when I moved to Massachusetts, I drove past a Nebraska cemetery on fire. Flames circled the tombstones like a shrine.

The hillside was smoking and black. But the stones remained bright against the darkening earth.

And though I did not return to see, I believe that eventually there was growth, the sweet smell of jasmine in the sun.

CONSTRUCTION

As spring shifts to summer, the wasps build a home. The slow papier-mâché construction domes fuller and fuller, like a womb, like a wound.

Soon it is impossible to escape the sound of the growing threat. Buzzing builds along with a bubble beneath the balcony where I sit to escape.

I want to escape the dark, the way the winter bleeds imperceptibly to spring, weighs hard and heavy. I want to escape this place, New England a home that has never felt my own, but now, at 35, seems to have claimed my future in a way for which I am neither willing nor prepared.

I want to escape my husband, who insists we stay here and call it home. We have become strangers here and the longer I stay, the more I feel a stranger to myself. I want to escape the house he insisted we buy as though this house would save our marriage.

The house is beautiful and we are lucky, but it is difficult to love a place where you feel trapped despite wildness all around. Nestled on several wooded acres next to a lake, we have an ivy-covered fence and red door like a cardinal in the snow, and space enough that we can run as fast and far as we want and still claim the ground beneath our feet. The woods encircle us, loneliness ricocheting through the clearing.

All spring I say the wasps are building a nest, call us to silence so we can hear the thrum. My husband says I imagine it, we will address it later, buying time by pouring me wine.

Building a nest begins with searching. A wasp queen determines a safe location—eaves, beams, abandoned sheds. Wasps take care to nest in safety, the nest delicate as origami or tissue paper flowers, a liability in places where the climate is cruel and indifferent.

Construction is an act of consumption. The queen searches for wood fiber from trees, logs, fences, cardboard left by the side of the road. She builds a home by stripping out the insides of another. Her jaws are strong and she chews fibers to a soft pulp.

To build the walls of her home she spits out what she has ground down to nothing. She empties herself to house others. The queen exists in an endless act of leaving, searching, only to be compelled back, called home.

❀

As a child, I helped my parents construct rooms inside of rooms.

Our home was small, my parents' desire for family endless. Over the years, my parents adopted five children to add to their three biological children. When I was thirteen, they adopted two-year-old twins, a boy and a girl. When I was nineteen, they adopted two- and three-year-old brothers. When I was twenty-one, they adopted a fifteen-year-old girl. They fostered countless others, took in homeless coworkers and stranded strangers, whole families of parents and children, bodies showing up on the doorstep, brushing against each other in the small space for as long as they needed until they left.

My parents shared an instinctual desire for expansion. Their childhoods had been marked by loss. My mother had been the youngest of alcoholic parents, hiding for safety when her father drank, wishing for a friend in that lonely house, promising one day to build a family of her own, to take in all the children whose faces looked frightened like hers in the mirror. My father's father was a cruel giant towering 6'9" over his 5'1 wife, a woman who birthed four boys and buried one, who hid her cancer until it was much too late to treat for fear that she would leave her children alone.

Family, therefore, must be constructed, my parents believed. This expansion, the careful art of survival. My half-brother was born the day before my father turned eighteen and the boy's biological mother left when he was still an infant. She simply walked out the door and never looked back. My father chose to stay and when my mother met him years later, she chose to become a step-mother when she was still a child, nineteen and raising an eight-year-old. They had me and my biological sister, and because the trauma of their childhoods pulsed like a hive, they opened their arms and the doors of our home, the foster care system eager to place as many children as they could, my parents eager to take in children who were difficult to place, those returned by other foster homes, children whose abuse records cast menacing shadows.

We had to sign forms each time a child joined the family, indicating that we knew they were dangerous, that they would likely try to hurt themselves and others, that they would try to set fire to the house or slit our throats in our sleep. The many shared hurts—my parents' loneliness and desperation, my siblings' trauma wailing from their mouths, my biological siblings' and my shared sense that we were somehow not enough—buzzed through the family, vibrating and hot.

Each time the family increased, the space decreased. My father built rooms inside the garage, cold and cramped with low ceilings so the garage door could creep up over you, remind you of how close you were to the exit. He built two rooms inside the family room, then divided these up again. Some rooms were small enough you could stretch your arms out and touch either side. Everywhere were walls, dividers, a sense the house was closing in.

I helped my parents because it was my duty. I lifted drywall, taped over seams, plastered and sanded them smooth. No matter how hard I tried, though, the places these makeshift walls came together showed, reminders that our whole was a collection of discarded parts.

My room was purple, dark and brooding like I increasingly felt as the walls moved closer all around me. I used a sponge roller to smooth texture across one wall so that the lilac looked like wings. When I looked at the walls through half-closed eyes or lids swollen from crying, they looked alive, fluttering and frantic.

When we outgrew the house, my parents built rooms and a bathroom in the old shed in the backyard. Beds nestled between boxes of old clothes and Christmas decorations, cobwebs and mice feces. The building was narrow with a low ceiling; we had to shrink to enter.

Sometimes my father and I drove past construction sites, the skeletons of houses bare and exposed. We entered and wandered the hollowed husks where other families would soon live. The rooms were bigger than ours, matching doors and floors. It was quiet on the sites and I could stretch out and touch nothing but possibility, call through the vast empty spaces to my father, who heard me in places where doors did not open onto doors, where you did not have to become smaller in order to belong.

◊

My earliest memory is of leaving one home in search of another.

In this memory, I am no more than three. I sit alone on the living room couch in the dark, surrounded by moving boxes. They seem like cardboard towers, stacked high in the sky. I look up at the reminder that this moment, this safety, this home is temporary.

Our house sits on several acres with fruit trees and vegetable patches, lush and fragrant. In the evenings, I wander outside with my father to watch him cut asparagus from the stalks and he says how lucky we are to live here. Years later he will speak of this house as the one that got away, the one he couldn't afford even if it were for sale instead of rent. He will recall the horse pasture across the street and the peacocks with their fanning color.

My parents left this house to purchase their first home, moving us further into the dusty backroads of California's Central Coast, back when home ownership was achievable even for those who had nothing. Even so, they barely made the monthly mortgage, leaving us with a roof over our heads and ramen in the pantry. My parents claimed a home in a town so small it was practically nonexistent, a few hundred people and not a single streetlight to brighten the dark. They knew not a soul, did not speak the language of their neighbors, but here they could buy into a dream even if the town was so dusty nothing would grow and they left dirty footprints anywhere they walked. They fled further and further up the California coast, away from clotted Los Angeles highways until they veined into the length of the state, away from their troubled homes, angry fathers and frightened mothers, looking for something they could afford to love.

In my memory, the room is dark except for the flicker of the TV, Garfield's body orange and hungry onscreen. I pass the time by hanging upside-down off the couch to watch the stacks of boxes appear like stalactites from the ceiling. I am alone, though surely my parents were just out of sight, packing our things, preparing to leave.

◊

At first, the wasp nest is shaped into a single domain. Soon, however, workers form wood pulp into hexagons, line the nest with geometry. They put up walls needed to hold eggs.

We call these divisions—rooms within rooms—cells.

Eventually the need to survive exceeds the space within the nest. Workers construct more rooms, more cells. There are approximately two hundred cells before the babies even arrive.

◊

Home has always felt temporary, my family shifting each season as more bodies arrived. We moved from home to home in search of more space, only to multiply and divide the rooms again.

Perhaps this is the reason forever has never seemed real—no sooner did our family stabilize than someone would leave, someone else new would arrive. What was family, home, but a rotation, a cycle of unfamiliarity and loss?

From an early age I learned the necessity of dismantling, the art of abandonment. I acquired the skill of rebuilding. I learned to divide, pack things away. There are rooms within rooms inside my memory, always the buzzing threat of danger inside.

Eventually, I learned to leave my poor hometown and all the hurting hearts held within our walls. I learned to leave because of the way my childhood closed in all around me—because of new walls and new siblings, scared babies who would not let me hold them turning into teens holding knives to themselves or to us, their violence the same as what coursed through our biological family's blood, the kind that made us drink too deeply, looking for escape, even from the places and people we claimed to love. I left first for college, then for graduate school, then again for a PhD, for a job, moving at the end of each academic year until every spring started to feel restless, a stirring inside of me that burst out each summer when I would abandon the home I'd made in order to begin again.

For me, perpetual motion felt urgent. Necessary for my survival. Necessary to ensure I didn't get trapped like the rest of my family.

It is impossible to escape the cycle imprinted on me. After so many years of welcoming strangers in, I am good at making friends, pulling them close and calling them family, equally good at abandoning them when the cycle completes itself. Then I pack up, make a new home elsewhere. I have made homes along the golden West Coast, deep in the heart of the Midwest, in the tangled forests of the East Coast, spanning the country in search of the safety I lost as a child. Of course, this sense of safety never lasts: a place has the comfort of home only when I know it is temporary.

Putting miles between me and my family is a pattern, an inevitability like the seasons. Each mile is a wall, a room divided.

When measured horizontally, the United States is 2,800 miles wide. My home in Massachusetts is 3,127 miles from my home in California.

I have found a way to lengthen the divide.

☙

Watercolors drip from the walls. A rose. A bright sun. A tree stretching to blue sky.

I am six years old and lonely in the playhouse my father builds for me. My new sister is on the way and my older brother has left and already I am understanding family as a series of arrivals and abandonments.

My father builds me a house in miniature, far grander than our own modest home. My playhouse has two stories and real carpet and a ladder to the loft above where there is a round porthole to glimpse my real house in case I feel too far away. The windows open and close and lock like the tiny front door because this home is all mine, my parents say, and our town is one where people deadbolt and no one plays in the front yard.

I am always pretending to live somewhere else. In the mirror I become another version of myself, one who lives in the fancy town where I go to school. At sleepovers with my fancy friends who aren't allowed to come to my town, my house, I insist we sleep on the trampoline like we can use the force of our weight to fly to the moon, or I crawl inside my friend's giant dollhouse, insist on sleeping there, though my legs are too long and my feet stretch out the back as if to run.

In my playhouse I paint a watercolor wasp on the wall because yellow is friendly and the wings look like the glass panels I peer through when I get lonely, solitude something to covet but also an ache.

When my real life gets too much—new siblings suddenly appearing, the men in my family shouting at the women, the overwhelming feeling of saying goodbye—I run away. I open my window and kick out the screen and fall to the ground and escape to my playhouse. I know it is only pretend. But when I lock the door behind me, sit in the dark, it feels like the hurt stops, and with it, time. It feels like I am the old me and the new me, two selves united, at least for a while.

I am a self divided across these two homes. And soon the real home will be too small, the dividing rooms pressing in all around and my parents talking about more children, so we will pack up and leave. We will move down the street to a house nearly double in size. We will try to sell it after only a year in search of another place to dismantle, except nobody will buy a maze of rooms and we can't afford to leave our town. There is a rotation of bodies over the years, some staying, some leaving so that I can't remember all their names, only the weight of hurting bodies and thrashing limbs, the feeling of being divided, the feeling that family, that home is never enough.

Now when I fly the long stretch back to California from the East, I go down the length of our small town's main street, back in time. I stare, small as a child, up the hill at our old house and my playhouse, still standing after all these years, faded sepia from so long left out in the sun.

◊

A nest constructed by a wasp colony will only last one season.

Each spring a queen forms new colonies, raising worker wasps to build the family a nest and provide food. Once the nest is large enough, she lays roughly fifty thousand eggs.

All summer, workers build the nest and care for the increasing family, venturing from the safety of the hive to procure food to feed the growing larvae. The adults do not eat. Instead, they rely on sweet secretions provided by their young. Wasps do not leave the nest for pleasure. They leave only to search, only when they must.

As summer ends, some young wasps develop into fertile males, some into fertile females that will become next year's queens. They flee the hive, swarm away from the colony in order to mate. In order to live, they must flee leave the home they have spent their lives constructing. The male drones die immediately, spent and purposeless, and as the weather grows colder, all the old workers and the old queen will die as well. The female wasps that fertilize their eggs are the only ones that will survive the winter.

The new queens are the only survivors, and they retreat under bark or into old buildings promising to build new colonies, new homes when the cycle calls. They do whatever it takes to ensure their survival.

◊

Ever since we met in college, my husband has been the sole constant in my life. In a family constantly reforming—siblings absorbed back by the system, those who stayed lost to drugs or incarceration—he is a permanence. He is the reminder that home does not need to shift beneath my feet.

For fifteen years, my husband has calmed and indulged my frantic search for belonging as I shift from place to place in search of education and distraction. He has made a home with me in California where we are both from, heat seeping from season to season so that it seems every moment is summer, an idyllic sort of living until the fires come and blacken the coast. He has made a home with me in the Midwest, the heartland about which my parents read aloud to me in *Little House on the Prairie* until the adoptions began and the stories stopped and I learned the family in my book were squatters stealing Indigenous homes. And he moved to the East Coast with me where my blood family first began, stripping away the insides of mines and themselves.

My husband and I have constructed our homes on the foundation of impermanence. I've long said I do not intend to ever inhabit one place too long, instead treating settling like the tides I came from, arriving only to retreat. And as we crossed the rough history of the Plains, then made our way to the extremes of New England's seasons, where I can't decide if I love or loathe the place, if it wants me at all, he has indulged my restlessness.

But now my husband wants to stay. He likes this place, finds Massachusetts fitting for us. He likes the way the state arcs into the sea as if trying to escape the country, yet curves as if to point back to our origin.

He has a right to a home of his own, one he can claim like I claim restlessness. Unlike many, my husband and I have options. We can choose a home that suits us. And I know this makes us lucky, that we can purchase not only a home but a home we like in a world where many cannot. So I agree. But at the same time, the process feels like a closing in all around me, a forever feeling that makes me want to run.

Our seller is difficult, the moving process prolonged. For months I am surrounded by boxes piled high. I feel the dead weight of winter creeping in. When we at last arrive at our new home, I look out the windows at the barren trees in the wooded clearing and see upturned cages.

◊

My father believed in marking, in placing your hands on the land to claim it. Each time we built—a playhouse, a patio, another room within a room—we held out our hands to the wet cement, froze ourselves in time. This way he said, we could find our ways home. There are many versions of myself buried.

As a child, I put my hand into wet cement, opened my palm as if to spread myself long across the land, the lines of my life already etched into my grasp. Reaching my fingers wide, I opened myself to the idea that I could be forever.

The cement hardened as soon as you put your hands into it. No sooner were you alive than you were frozen, like how your reflection was already behind you, like animals in tar or amber, behind museum glass frozen in time.

A home was not our own until we marked it. For each new sibling, my father poured new concrete, called us outside to place our hands together, solidify our bond. Eventually, though, there were too many. Some of my siblings do not exist in my father's makeshift geologic record, so perhaps this is why they do not call us family despite a lifetime together, why they will not accept a phone call much less a hug, why they leave their palm prints bruised across our bodies (and their own), why they run into the sea or the streets, seeking the buzz of addiction, the sting of a needle.

When I moved to the Midwest, I saw the ways the bison had scarred the prairie with their heavy trails along ridges and river valleys, pushing their shaggy shoulders into the rock, leaving their palms long across the Plains. They marked the land with their survival.

Now in New England, the coast is littered with scrimshaw, crude attempts to lay hands on the land. For a price, you can purchase the bones of those who did not survive, or did so with scars, carved by sailors desperate and lonely for home even as they were compelled to the sea's uncertainty.

&

Defending the nest is the responsibility of the female wasp. Male wasps do not have stingers.

Unlike bees, who can sting only once, wasps are capable of stinging repeatedly. They can injure endlessly if it means protecting the hive.

When wasps are in trouble, they alert the family, send pheromone signals to the others that the group is in danger.

&

My husband and I move into the house a few days before the start of 2020. He promises that, with time, I will call this place home. It is beautiful, I can't deny, a few acres resting at the edge of a lake and surrounded by protected wetlands, deer and foxes playing in the yard, great blue herons swooping low to come to nest. But the neighboring wetlands mean the air is filled with wasps who strip wood from the railing and deck, chew it up to spit it out.

And then we are trapped before we have even fully arrived, because this is the year no one goes out. The world is frozen, all of us hurting and hating and working and schooling from home. It is also the year the siblings who stayed with our family are in and out of psychiatric facilities and jail, are smoking and snorting again though they had just stopped. It is the year I see old foster siblings on the news, breaking into homes to beat strangers bloody. It is a year at once unprecedented and also full of familiar threats.

The news buzzes with danger, with death and destruction. We are desperate to travel through time, to go back before or to move to an after that seems impossible. The chaos spares no one: it infiltrates every home, the whole world united in collective trauma. I busy myself by collecting shells from the nearby shore, by removing the front fence to let in the wild. I dig up the concrete holding the posts. They are buried deep, and I dig further and further so I can make it all come crashing down.

All spring the danger grows, wasps spiraling overhead, and soon my husband cannot ignore the way the yard vibrates like a pulse, the wasps winding their ways into the eaves above our bed.

They are building their home inside our own.

The month I turn thirteen I become an adult. Two new siblings arrive overnight, already the promise of more, and my role as dutiful oldest daughter hardens, trapping me inside.

My parents work long hours to pay for this new family we cannot afford and now I babysit each day, cook breakfasts and lunches, clean up after each meal. I am expected to wash the children's laundry, bathe and dress the young ones, potty-train the babies and help the others with their homework. My parents are busy, busy, finding new children to love, new bodies to bring home, so I am not allowed to leave. I cannot go to parties or field trips. No more sleepovers or summer camp. I am to stay in the house, hot from the California sun, swelling in the triple digits inside because we cannot afford air conditioning and so we keep the curtains closed instead, all of us shrouded in darkness, the heat from so many bodies vibrating.

I try to love them, to love myself. I reach out my arms to the babies and they rush in, calling me *mother* because they have had many mothers and they do not know which one is real anymore. But often they stiffen at my embrace, or turn their backs, or slap my face. This, my parents insist, is part of building a home. So I build a wall each time a child arrives and exposes himself or tries to climb in bed with me at night, each time they shout "bitch" before starting a fire or slitting a tire or hiding knives in their mattresses, each time my parents say they need to escape from the chaos and leave me to look after the children at home.

I hold very still in that house, hoping that if I freeze, I will not get stung. I go dormant like a wasp in winter.

School is the only time I get to leave my life. I am smart so I am allowed to escape my dusty town by going to the school several towns away, where everyone has only one sibling and doors do not open onto other doors. At school I can almost convince people I belong until they notice the holes in my shoes or see my mother dropping me off with a van full of wailing children.

At lunch I sit with my middle school friends and I hope no one hears hunger buzzing in my stomach and I wonder what it feels like to have food enough, to be enough. My friends here have families that last more than a season and I listen to them talk with envy but also feeling that I couldn't live in their tidy homes and culs-de-sac without wanting to run.

I shift my weight in the California sun, leaning on my hand to prop myself up. I am surrounded by all the friends that will feel like family until we graduate. We girls are busy with the work of gossip and worry, the boys droning all around.

When I feel the sting, it is already too late. It is done, the wasp wriggling in my palm. My hand got too close; it threatened the insect's survival.

All day my hand aches, but when I show my parents that night, the mark is invisible. They tell me it is not possible to hurt that much from an injury no one can see.

◊

It is difficult to rid ourselves of danger.

When my husband realizes the nest is swelling like a womb, like a wound above us, he senses my fear and wraps himself around me like he has these many years. We go on long drives and I get lost in places I don't recognize, feel a sense of relief in running, even if it is to nowhere, even if we must always return, to our home, to our compromise.

We need an exterminator, but the world is closed and no one can come. It is late in the season and the colonies have already multiplied and begun new nests, bulbs hanging from the eaves like ominous Christmas ornaments. We buy many cans of spray and discuss how to rid ourselves of the past.

I call my parents to ask about how to own a home. We discuss infestation. I have not seen my parents during this long year we have all been trapped inside and I miss them, even miss the California home that never felt like mine, a home now swarming with children I do not recognize, my many siblings' many children.

From inside the house, I watch my husband approach the nests, worrying he will be hurt, that he does not understand how difficult it is to escape a swarm. The chemicals he sprays are thick like smoke, dense and gray so that the image of him seems a black and white photo, gone diffuse with time.

I feel guilty about hurting the wasps, about destroying their home. They have worked so hard to build them. They only wanted to survive.

It takes many sprays and many days, but at last the nests are wet and soft, only a few homeless creatures spiraling the entrances.

The nests fall easily to the ground. They take no effort at all to crumble.

LESSONS IN CARTOGRAPHY

LESSON ONE: CARDINAL DIRECTIONS

A compass rose looks like a stained-glass sun, arrows pointing out possibilities in precision, intervals spaced by half, then half of half. Sometimes the rose consists of four points: north, south, east, west. Sometimes it has a midpoint between each one. Other times, it includes these four directions and about a dozen others, each arrow carefully shaded half-black, half-white—as though direction were that easy.

I used to like my compass rose with just the four base parts, none of these intermediate directions. But the older I get, the more I need something intermediary when things don't go according to plan—or more importantly, when what I desire is not easily governed.

When I was twenty-four, I left California, the place I'd always known, to move to Nebraska, a place I'd never been, the craggy coast shrinking in my rearview mirror as I headed due east. I was heading to a version of myself I was still writing, one with a PhD and opportunities beyond my small town. I followed my careful life plan, but though I didn't yet realize it, I was heading to some intermediary position on the compass.

What concerned me was the way I was leaving my position as insider to become an outsider, leaving the West to go backwards. If Manifest Destiny governs this country, which prides itself on reaching the Pacific, why was that ocean a blurred line behind me? John Gast's *American Progress* shows Columbia in her white robes, golden hair, book in hand, tiptoeing—no, floating—toward the ocean, bringing light with her, driving settlers towards their apparent destiny. Never mind the way the animals, a bear in one corner of the canvas, bison in the other, flee from her. No matter that Indigenous people trudge before her, their figures overshadowed by her imposing foot.

What concerned me was that I was leaving in defiance of cardinal direction. Soon I would travel far enough away that the ocean would sink behind the curve of the earth. Like most people, I had to leave a place to realize I loved it. It wasn't until I drove in the opposite direction that I first felt an ache for the coast, that particular strip of land, wondered how to find home somewhere else.

LESSON TWO: SCALE

As I moved across space—pillows, boxes of books, a spatula rattling in the backseat—the landscape was different than my maps promised. A map represents a region of earth or heavens on a plane; it is a way of making the world compact and easily foldable. But when I unfolded a map during meals or at a quick rest stop, shifted my eyes from the road to the paper stretched across my steering wheel, I found the mountain wrinkles and river squiggles didn't match what surrounded me or what was ahead.

Maps utilize scale, a ratio of distance on parchment or digital screen to the distance across great sweeps of land. If the images depicted on the map are small enough to ignore the Earth's curvature, then the scale is constant. A constant scale is less deceptive. If, however, a map covers larger areas—say, a large geographical landmark or the entire globe spinning on a metal axis on a desk somewhere—distortion occurs as the sphere must become the plane. It is impossible to create a map with a perfect scale.

On my map, the Sierra Nevadas were a few jagged triangles, wrinkled like pantyhose, sprawling over two states. The states were precisely boxed, as though a child new to crayon might be instructed to color within the boundaries. The map provided elevation and a route but said nothing of the way my car would slow at the climb, the way I'd be compelled to stare up, up.

On my map, the Grand Canyon was a thick line, a spatter of numbers. But when I parked and made my way according to the signs, I was breathless and fearful at the sight. The canyon stretched further down than anything I'd imagined or would be able to imagine after, shades shifting with the layers of sediment, watercoloring through time. I tried to peer down to the river at the bottom, but the depth made me dizzy and I wanted to swoon, crawl along my belly to the edge and stare a good long while at the rock ridges and clefts. I stayed several hours walking from rim to rim and back, awed and a little stomach-sick by the permanence and force the gash suggested.

My map had hinted at none of this.

Lesson Three: Roadmaps

A roadmap looks like a series of veins under elderly skin—a lifetime of stories and scars. Look at a roadmap and you'll see where the blood flows, where it is thickest and where it tributaries out to the limbs. Look at a roadmap and you'll see where the veins of a country or a county, a state or a city, intersect and hub.

Roadmaps show major highways and roads. They show airports and railroad tracks. Cities and points of interest. Roadmaps are for planning where to go, usually when you don't plan to stay.

My eyes couldn't keep the roads straight and soon the lines seemed to move rather than simply sitting stagnant. There was an interstate number when I drove through Utah, but the number didn't matter—what mattered was that I was on a red vein, the blue vein of the Colorado River beside me. The map revealed a thinner road too, an offshoot declared "191." This interstate, the map said, would lead to Moab, a point of interest.

What I knew of Moab was from photos, orange and red rocks that seemed as though they would leave a chalky residue on my hands if I were to run my palms across. What I knew of Moab was that there was a curve of rock called Delicate Arch, where the wind blew through so deliberately it left a rainbow of stone, an upside-down smile like the quizzical faces of tourists who tried to figure out how it was done.

The roadmaps did not tell me this. Nor did they tell me the way this place was covered by ocean during the Pennsylvanian period, was once ocean dunes and floodplains. The roadmaps did not tell me that white-throated swifts nest on top of the arch during the summer, the down at their throats breaking up the slick black of their bodies. The way the wind felt like air from a dryer vent, the way the dirt made its way into the tread of my shoes, leaving a trail for days afterwards. The way my hands, cramped from clutching the wheel as I made my way to my new home in Nebraska, eased at the sight of the Colorado Plateau, a rock formation that has seen little faulting or folding within the last 600 million years. The way we tourists stared, mouths slightly open at this place we did not understand.

Lesson Four: Data
When looking at a map, discerning how to get from here to there and quickly, we say we are reading. On my trip I read books late at night in motels, pausing to peer out the windows at my tiny car burdened with my things. I spent my last night on the road in Denver, Colorado, peering first at my book, then at my maps, then out the window at the Mile High City, which, like all my stops on this route, seemed different than the maps had promised. When I read my book, I was mindful of the syntax, of a specific word. I stopped and reread and thought, "Yes. That's it exactly." I stared at the ceiling and rolled sentences over in my mouth like bright berries.

I didn't do this with the maps. I opened them and refolded them. I sharpened the creases with my nail. I thought, "This is a lie." I spilled tea, left a brown stain across Montana.

Until this journey, I'd never stopped to parse maps, to think of the way a map's contexts can be extended, the way the map can be read through various lenses. We rarely stop to think "Yes. That's exactly it," or more correctly, "No. That's all wrong." I, like most, referred to a map for numbers, raw data, the most convenient route across a given latitude or longitude.

The imposed grid system of latitudes for north and south directions, longitudes for east and west directions, measures distances over the Earth's surface. It has been used since first suggested in 300 B.C. by Hipparcus and was standardized by world mapmaking in 1884. The Prime Meridian, 0° longitude, took years and death and millions in reward to achieve. Britain appointed the first royal astronomer in 1675, building an observatory to improve sea navigation and to find a way to map the heavens so man could sail across the seas, every minute important in navigation, the data precious. Years later, however, there was still no progress. In 1707, over two thousand men were killed in a sea disaster. By 1714, Parliament had offered a reward of £20,000 reward (the equivalent of about $3 million today), but the prize went unclaimed for nearly sixty years until John Harrison, an unknown carpenter, managed to invent the marine chronometer that would accurately measure longitude and change cartography. Now Google Maps will tell you how far to drive without needing to know these things; satellite imaging will show you precisely what a motel or rest stop diner looks like. Google Earth makes the entire world accessible and while GPS navigation systems display a highlighted map, looking at the image isn't necessary because a calm voice simply commands the driver, "Left turn ahead."

This ease of mapping and movement means most people don't know how far a mile is or what direction a river flows or that the Prime Meridian, like most mapping tools and conventions, is arbitrary. That despite this arbitrariness, we give prime meridians to celestial bodies, trying to impose form and order on moons, ringed Saturn, reddened Mars, to prove our power over place through mapping.

Maps, in theory, tell us how to know land, how to move across the sea when we cannot see the land at all, yet most of us don't know the fundamentals of cartography. All we've got to tell us about place is data, but numbers are stoic and clinical, seemingly simplistic when fit into a system dating back to the Babylonians and revised again and again by the likes of Johannes Werner, Ptolemy, Newton. And while the data makes "sense," while the system has certainly been synthesized, the numbers are meaningless—or rather, easily manipulated, imposed by humans, cartographers who can render the world in any way they choose.

Lesson Five: Political Maps

If we do understand maps as a way of imposing order on a landscape, as the history of Magellan, Cortez, Robert de LaSalle, Daniel Boone, Kit Carson and others, of man vs. nature, of expansion and conquest, aren't all our maps political?

A so-called political map does not show roads, or physical features, or topography. Instead, a political map indicates state and national boundaries, major cities, capital cities marked with a circumscribed star. A political map tells who is in control and how far this control reaches.

When Jefferson ordered Manifest Destiny, he wanted maps to establish a United States claim of discovery to the Pacific Northwest—an American presence before any other. The maps and journal accounts—scientific data on plants and animals, climates and seasons—was documentation to prove knowledge of place and thus ownership. He sent the expedition across the continent to write the story of America and erase anything that countered this narrative.

The early maps of John Meares, James Cook, Alexander Dalrymple, and Philippe Buache sought to do the same. Their maps stretch out on fanciful scrolls, more attention given to the brightly colored figures framing the maps than to the places themselves. The land seems secondary when surrounded by men on horses, burning villages, exotic women in the right-hand corner. There was no need, these early maps suggest, to represent rivers running aortic through a place, or the endless sky, or Indigenous communities when the artist could instead render images of a sea dragon, a phoenix, settlers teaching Indigenous children to read in English.

Strangest about these old maps are the ways they offer alternate views of place. My concept of the world spins and changes when I see these maps, some with land cut open and spread across a plane in a way that seems broken, some rendering places I've never seen with so much detail I feel disoriented, some with the world so small in comparison to the surrounding figures it seems secondary to the people and to artistic flourishes. No matter the perspective, however, something remains the same: thick borders outline the land, holding in continental coasts, dancing along the edge of a territory, demarcating ownership.

In Nebraska museums, Indigenous maps represent my new home on the Plains differently. Lean Wolf's map showing the course he took on a horse raid from the Hidatsa village at Fort Berthold to the Sioux Valley at Fort Buford is lively and organic, shapes and story free of the clinical calculation of the conqueror, images and narrative that do not require readers to refer to an explanatory key, to defer to the cartographer's grand vision.

White Bird's painting of the Battle of Little Bighorn, too, is a map free from data gleaned from a compass or conqueror. While some may argue the painting is not a map because it does not outline edges and limitations, it will tell you much about the place. Look at this map to witness movement and history, the way place is shaped and scarred by human contribution and violence.

LESSON SIX: LEGEND

A legend is the guide to the system. A legend uses words, phrases, or colors to explain the way the world is depicted. Grassland is pale pink. Streams a steady blue line. Bare land is yellow.

One must read the map—the world, in essence—through the cartographer's eyes. Rarely can you understand the map without the legend, without the cartographer's direction and control. The land changes with time—places grind along fault lines, the sea laps at shifting shore lines, we dam rivers or strip away mountains until what's left looks like empty ribs—so maps are the stories that persist, the stories we seek out to see our roots, to know backward into how we arrived, why we are.

But what is to be done when the cartographer's legend does not satisfy? What happens when the stories might not be true?

As I left Denver and made my way to Nebraska, the mountains dipping low to the Plains, I found no map whose legend seemed truth. The maps I followed showed restrooms and picnic spots, gas stations and coffee stops, but none of the texture I experienced. A river on the map was just a line, the highway overshadowing it according to the map's legend. But the river I saw stretched for miles, ran further and faster than the highway, eclipsed the water towers that reached toward the sky high above. In reality, the river defied legend, layers of trees growing alongside the water, bowing low to greet the edge, bright chokecherries ripe with astringency, mosquitoes rhyming along with the sound.

Follow early maps of the outbound route Lewis and Clark took and you'll move along the river as well, from Camp Dubois up through the corner of Nebraska, up the Missouri through South Dakota and through states one by one to the Pacific. The Niobrara, Cheyenne, Knife and Milk rivers branch off as though they are running away from the cartographers. The expedition arrived in Omaha, Nebraska in late summer, just as I arrived years later. Legends on these Lewis and Clark maps are myth, the mythos of the West, of progress, of

Columbia marching back toward the way I came. Legends are the way the men made sense of what they saw, mapped it along with a story they hoped others would believe to be true. Read their journals and you'll find the daily accounts of men looking to write the world onto a foldable space.

LESSON SEVEN: PHYSICAL MAPS

I'd thought driving into the Heartland would feel more decisive, like I'd realize what the place meant when I got there. Months of researching my new home, using satellite imaging to take me right onto the main streets and looking at tourist maps to pinpoint where to shop and eat had me feeling as though I could arrive and simply reorient myself.

But the drive left me uncertain, the supposed accuracy of the maps negated by my experience. Physical maps promise flatland, leave the page smooth and unblemished. In doing so, they neglect the midwestern sky, which is as fierce and terrifying during a summer storm as it is awesome when calm, the way it domes across the expanse of space, curves higher and further than it could anywhere else in the country. To be on the Plains is to be aware of the sky, to reorient your gaze upward, to willingly conceive of yourself as smaller.

To be on the Plains is also to honor a long history. Fossil records place sandhill cranes in Nebraska for over nine million years, the birds returning each spring to witness the landscape change, for they've seen the creation of the Platte River 10,000 years ago, the bison giving way to cattle, prairie grass giving way to corn.

And we are changing the fundamental nature of the place—indeed, of place itself—now, altering physical landscapes through the stubborn nature of our will. Maps drawn up by the Lewis and Clark expedition have long since ceased to be true, if they ever were, the physical nature of place permanently altered or disrupted with the passage of time and our contemporary maps outdated at an ever-quickening pace.

Now some physical maps include manmade elevations or points of interest, dams or bridges, fast food restaurants and Starbucks drive-thrus. Cartographers use these elements to order a place, defining experience for the traveler before they've even left the car. We deal with temporality rather than physicality; we know a place by the markers we've designed rather than by those which have defined that place throughout history.

I wonder what our maps will look like long after the restaurants have been replaced, freeways rerouted, land smoothed or terraced or concreted. Our sense of place and permanence shifts so quickly, I wonder if we'll be look back at our satellite images the way we look at old maps, bright flags and ships moving in the margins, drawing the eye away from the place and towards the mapmaker's name calligraphed across the corner.

LESSON EIGHT: THE CARTOGRAPHER

The cartographer presumably knows place best, for whom else but the most intimate steward of the land to map a place, to tell the lifeblood of a landscape, the heartbeat of a region?

Like God, the cartographer gives us a world, maps our existence in and on it. The cartographer sets the map's agenda, as though the map had an order of business or some underlying motive. A well-designed map, according to American geographer Alan MacEachren, "is convincing because it implies authority." Readers of maps, therefore, must believe in the power and truth of the mapmaker over that inherent to the region, to the land itself.

The cartographer tells us how to know a place, chooses the traits to be mapped, chooses what is relevant. The cartographer reduces the complexity of characteristics to be mapped, orchestrates elements to best convey a message to an audience. In cartographer's terms, these decisions are called *projections, generalizations*. In a writer's terms, they are called *editing*.

As with so many of many of our interests and contributions, there is a certain hubris in this editing, a sense of unearned arrogance and accomplishment. Look at maps from the 1600s, 1700s, and the 1800s and you'll see the cartographer's name declared. Look at the border, the frame around the map embellished to appear nearly as important as that which it holds. Look at the banner proclaiming the one who commissioned the map. Look at the craft, for that's certainly what cartography is: a crafting of place. As with most things, those with power do the writing.

Competition is apparent, too, cartographers earning their place in cultural memory. Early map-makers—Herman Moll, Nicolas de Fer—used to steal from one another, one map appearing innocuously in another, engravers taking credit for the expedition and artistry. In 1806, as Clark went east to establish the legend of the empty West, he collected Indigenous maps to fill in the blanks where his own maps fell short.

Mid-century American cartographer, Arthur H. Robinson, says if a map is not properly designed it "will be a cartographic failure," that out of everything cartographers must do, "map design is the most complex." According to Robinson, a cartographer owes his audience a superior design and scope. A cartographer must teach. With cartography came the printing press and mass production, magnetic compass and telescope, lithograph and GPS. Now the cartographer has new ways of imaging and recording—satellites that show what a city looks like down to a fine blade of grass, three-dimensional topographies, resource maps that change with the stock market.

What is superior design, superior scope? How do we frame a landscape, the stories it tells?

FINAL LESSON: DEEP MAPS

When I came to Nebraska, people told me roadmaps would be simple, that the city of Lincoln was designed as a grid, easy to follow and commit to memory. But roadmaps didn't tell me I'd have difficulty adjusting to the few lanes of traffic instead of six- and eight-lane freeways. When I came to Nebraska, the population maps promised Lincoln was not a large city, but I found the freeways and city center crowded compared to the dirt roads and one-stoplight town I'd called home. When I came to Nebraska, I had another type of legend: Buffalo Bill and his Wild West show, visions of *Little House on the Prairie*, and the fantasy of Dorothy and Toto wandering the Plains in black and white.

A final lesson, it seems, comes from looking at the way we've recorded land and its ownership, its physical attributes and resources and the manmade marks we've added, and noticing what we've left out or altered or erased altogether. Noticing what we never knew. Traditional maps did nothing to usher me from outsider to insider, said nothing to me of the history or soul of the place. All they provided was the patina—no grain or root.

There is something to be said for travel along secondary roads, for avoiding large cities and tourist points of attraction. Something to be said for getting to know place in ways beyond the map, devoid of the nostalgia that so often makes up our understanding of place, of country, of legend. There is something to be said for exploring a region regardless of scale or conquest, to know place not horizontally across a plane, but vertically, using geographical and natural history, stories and folklore, archaeology and weather to travel through time.

Deep maps do not feign objectivity or claim authority like conventional cartography, nor do they imply who has the ability to describe a place. Everyone can be a cartographer. We can be from more than one place, can find a stake in a new place or one we are only visiting. Roaming makes coming home richer, for when we explore places beyond our understanding and experience, we see connections between places we never imagined—say, for me, between California and Nebraska—and the depth of history and value in each.

When I arrived in the Midwest I was lonely for California, lonely for the shore and the salt of an ocean breeze, lonely for vineyards dotting hillsides. I was so lonely I was willing to reach out to an unfamiliar space, as most travelers are. When we travel somewhere new, we open ourselves up to what it will provide. What I found was that it isn't hard to love the Midwest; it isn't hard to love any space if you are mindful.

It took several years to begin to understand Nebraska: how glaciers moved over this space, smoothing it and depositing rich soil, how once megafauna—woolly mammoths with arced tusks, giant sloths and saber-toothed tigers—walked the plains, and then the buffalo, moving seamlessly as the grasses grew and cured, Indigenous communities following with the seasons. I still feel as though I've only started to learn about prairie grass, the way the roots stretch underground for a braided eternity, the way fire fuels their growth. Only started to appreciate the way a storm leaves the sky Coke-bottle-green, the way you can feel a tornado in your bones, or the premonition of snow, only started to appreciate the way this place demands a love affair with the weather.

In Nebraska, I made my map by figuring out the roads on my own, taking the longest route from here to there to see something unfamiliar. My map included the small towns not listed on other maps. It included bee-keeping on a hill, a prairie burn. I made my map by talking to people whose families had lived there for generations, learning about the sorrows of this place, the historical and contemporary cruelties against Indigenous populations, the Easter Blizzard of 1873 and the Night of the Twisters, the KKK presence in the 1920s and 30s, and the murder of Brandon Teena.

I made my map each afternoon when, no matter the season, I walked three or four miles along a trail behind my home. The trail stretched the length of the city and though walking was something I'd never done in California, I found that my new position in this place asked quietly for it, asked for me to come and be in the space, a part of it rather than an observer.

My map was the way I first cut through a neighborhood, dappled light through the branches, two little girls riding bikes and whispering "hi." The way the trail appeared behind the neighborhood as though the city were vanished, fuchsia flowers looking like stars, a slender gopher frozen outside his hole, bright eyes pointed up with his nose to the sun, cardinals with sharp beaks and calls, a black squirrel running the same length of branch each afternoon, and glittering insects, some larger than an outstretched finger. The ways things smelled as the seasons shifted, the sight of rabbits brown against the stark snow, hidden in the dirt when the melt came. My map was the way this trail led for miles on either side, as far from my home, as far into place as I wanted. My map was the way I ignored the mile markers to walk deeper.

DESCENDANT

Darkness comes quick. He is swallowed whole, gulped into the cavernous mouth of the earth. As he descends, the entrance shines bright above, a pinprick of light like a beacon calling him home. He holds his breath and counts how many steps it takes before the sun disappears.

It feels like he is inside something living. He smells dirt and wet, hears the heavy breath of the men heading underground to work the same shifts they've worked their entire lives, the same shifts their fathers and grandfathers worked before. His own breath is shallow and expectant. Eager. Afraid.

At sixteen, he does not sign a driver's license. Instead, he signs the paperwork to mine coal. He practices signing his name beforehand, letters looping into oblivion, a balloon on a string drifting to nowhere.

Like the canary in a cage at his side, the boy grows quiet the further underground he travels. Eventually, the lanterns give out and he stoops in the dark, hunched like a question.

🔥

Years after his death, my grandfather remains a mark on our family. I have no memory of him that doesn't involve his impending demise.

The women in my family flit around to ensure his comfort after the stroke. They flinch far too often. They do not look him in the eye while spooning food into his mouth, wiping him clean.

My mother loves him most, asking "Daddy, Daddy, what can I get you?" and bringing him glass after glass of water. He has an unquenchable thirst. He does not say thank you, but when he gets angry, which is often, he shouts, slurs, spittle flying like the objects on the table he clears with his cane.

I am ten and do not understand why this man is so angry, so thirsty. Why even his fingers slant as if they are trying to escape his grip, his very hands.

My grandparents live in a place called Heritage Ranch, and each twisting drive further into the rural backroads feels as though it leads my parents and me to our legacy. There is a marker halfway on the drive there, a large rock like a chimney in the sky. Years ago, they used to hang men from this rock as a warning to trespassers.

I shiver at the thought when we pass, lean into turns that curve like a noose. I love the solitude, the neighbors out of sight, but I fear how far it is from civilization, how loud any of us would have to cry out for help.

At the end, my grandfather looks like Gollum, all bone and sinew, gnarl and scowl. He stores his teeth in a jar on the bathroom sink and they grin at me as I pee, as if to make me ashamed. I see my face—and within it, my mother and grandmother's faces, their fears—staring back.

In memory, my grandfather curls in his seat like an inquiry, a grand inquisition, rolling Werther's butterscotch candies around his toothless maw. He sucks the candies until they are tasteless, spitting out the colorless husks for my grandmother to clean.

◊

The boy coats his throat to keep from choking in the mines. Candy wrappers rustle in his pocket. He is constantly gagging on soot, on dust, on his own tongue. His eyes burn, his muscles sting. His toenails fall off in his tight work boots and when he removes his socks at night, the half-moons scatter across the floor like stars.

There are few certainties underground, so he sucks hard candies for a sense of control. He chooses sour to remind him of brightness: cherries, limes.

A layer of soot rings both his eyes and the wrinkles at his knuckles. He leaves dirty footprints when he walks, stains girls who let him paw their breasts on Saturday nights. Each morning, he and the others take turns adding to the stinking hole with their black shit.

This is a small price to pay, he thinks. He blames himself for his mother's death. When he was a child, he stayed out too long in the Pennsylvania snow one evening, his mother waiting too long for him at the open front door. He remembers her slim figure haloed by the porchlight, calling out his name to light up the dark.

Pneumonia is what killed her, but the boy blames his desire to fly. When he raced his sled, he thought only of the wind on his cheeks.

After her death, he believed descent a fitting punishment. When he left school to work the mine, the workers called his name too, the syllables of his very existence ricocheting in the cavern until they disappeared into nothing.

He learned to make a living by hollowing the mountains. But to claim a mountain's strength you must succumb, collapse, make yourself small—like a child, a rat, a mole, like the animals whose bones littered the miners' path in the dark. Going underground requires contortion. You surrender strength. Sometimes, when trapped, you must break your very bones in order to become free.

The chamber walls became a second skin, held dust slick against his back until he believed his own soul filthy, circling black down the drain.

"Be careful," his father said the first day the boy returned from work to place his wages on the table, a constellation of silver coins. Still, he took the boy's coins, walked away with the sky jangling in his pocket.

Over the years, the boy was forever trying to wet his throat, coughing, sputtering, forever trying to keep from drying up.

Generations of my family on my mother's side made their livings from scraping out the insides of the earth, using the innards to set the world on fire. We stole the earth away from itself, left only enough to hold up the roof so we might escape.

And then we went back, stole what coal remained to hold up the mine ceiling. We called it "retreat" mining as though we were at war.

We backed out of the danger towards the light, watched the world cave in on itself. More than once, the roof collapsed on men and we breathed a sigh of relief it wasn't us.

It is no wonder we broke under the weight of this contradiction. Our children thrown to the depths; our bodies told they existed to submit.

🔥

He cried after he threw her, watching her body slump against the wall, tilting the garish 1970s floral painting in the dining room. When the whiskey went wrong, he hissed at demons he saw hiding in the canvas. It hurt to look at the orange flowers, so bold in their brush strokes, so like the sun he'd grown up lacking. When he was especially hurting, the light seemed an attack.

The boy became a man in the dark. Then he chased the light, moving to Hollywood, a city where he crushed stars beneath his feet and the lights shined so bright there was no night. He married a girl who preened for him and crooned her love and bore his children. He escaped from underground hoping to become a pilot, hoping to transcend the heavy pull of gravity and to fly straight to the heart of the sun. But he was only ever a mechanic, confined to fixing flying machines, looking up at their bellies from his back.

Liquor took the cruel glare off the sun. Whiskey wet his ever-dry throat, warmed his stomach until he could laugh. But when she stood in front of the painting, his wife appeared to him as a ghost, the specter of his mother come back, demons lurking behind. He pushed her aside to drink deeper.

He did not spy his daughter—my mother—hiding atop the dining room chairs, tucked out of sight. She learned to crouch like a miner, to keep the lights off.

🔥

In *Hell*, one of William Blake's 1824 watercolor illustrations inspired by Dante's *The Divine Comedy*, a man stands over the body of a lost love, bright sun like a spotlight overhead.

The dead figure's soul lifts overhead into a tunnel sweeping up into the sky before spiraling down underground. The soul smokes and plumes, all swirl and stroke, multiplying as it descends until the tunnel is filled with dozens of shadowy figures fighting for space, breath, crouched and creeping over one another, reaching hands up towards the light.

It is clearly the underworld, as Blake's title denotes. The curving tunnel, the crowded bodies, the choking smoke.

I cannot recall a recent family memory that does not involve intoxication.

A few years ago, my father got drunk and high and fell, saw stars from his daze on the kitchen floor.

The last time I went home for Christmas, many years ago, one of my sisters got so drunk she fell, punched her boyfriend who punched her back—though no one ever talked about it. After she snapped his glasses in half, he wept blindly, incoherent on the front lawn, as another drunk sister walked her pit bull down the dimly-lit street, the dog's back arched and bristled.

For years, one of my brothers made his living selling drugs, and he taught this to our two youngest brothers, who are now in high school—that is, when they aren't drifting in and out of police custody. They earned felonies and arrest warrants before driver's licenses, kept homemade pipes and syringes in their room next to their Matchbox cars.

As for my mother, I've learned not to call her after 5:00 p.m. When I do, there is a softness to her voice, one where the borders bleed like they have given up, like the stress of being a girl who watched her father drink and shout and slap, who is now a mother watching her children drink and shout and slap, has finally become too much. I think she drinks because only that liquid descent softens the painting of her life until the sharp edges blur, until things look watercolor.

She didn't always. Though she drank occasionally when I was growing up, she didn't slip into sadness the way she does now, weeping at restaurants and telling strangers her problems because she must stay silent at home. Sometimes I do not recognize this woman who tiptoes around her addicted children lest they turn their anger on her, who crouches like a miner and turns off the lights. I miss my mother. She feels smaller, hunched to me. Though she is aging, I see the little girl she was—lonely and fearful, perched in the dining room, waiting for disaster.

With eight children, it is hard to gather our entire family together. In the fall of 2019, we came close and managed to get seven of the siblings together after my niece was diagnosed with a rare cancer. All my siblings got high in the restaurant parking lot, balancing their babies on their hips as they passed around the pipe. Later, at the table, everyone laughed too loud despite nursing old wounds, spilled wine across the table, drove off too drunk. The only sibling besides me who didn't join in was my youngest brother, his drug probation ankle monitor flashing like a beacon in the black.

🔥

The creature stares the viewer down, bone and sinew, gnarl and scowl. He gives a toothless snarl. In Henri Fuseli's 1871 oil painting *The Nightmare*, a woman in a long white gown rests splayed—slumber or stupor?—across a divan, her clothing and body glowing with light. She is helpless to the creature sitting atop her chest, the darkness creeping close.

While the woman's pale body lights up the center, the background is barely visible through the blackness. The creature's shadow looms above her. On the table sit a series of half-empty bottles, amber with spirits.

🔥

After my grandfather's death, my grandmother bought a golden bird and crooned to it like she never could when her husband was alive. He liked the house quiet so he could hear his baseball games and talk to the radio.

When she wanted the bird quiet, she placed a cover over its cage, shrouding it in shadow. But the bird whistled in the dark.

My grandmother did not drink very much, but she did smoke her whole life, her mouth puckered from holding both a cigarette and silence between her lips.

One day her bird, the feathered thing, cried out, choked on her smoke, and fell dead from its perch.

🔥

My grandfather suffocated to death. He died of pneumonia like his mother, his lungs coal black, coated from his time in the mines.

Trace our family tree back far enough and you'll find generation after generation dead from mining America, mining England, scooping out the land and leaving it—and with it, themselves—empty. Our family tree grew from this underground misery. It is no wonder we continue to suffer similarly, to fear confinement and caving-in, the canary echoing through the chambers of our hearts.

Plants buried in arid soil struggle to survive. We are no different. Look at our family tree and you see a trunk heavy with rot, limbs struggling to sprout green shoots. To descend is to go against the natural order. To witness your own burial.

As my family falls apart, I can't help but wonder if what we thought we buried is rising to the surface.

🔥

During the first few months of the pandemic, my mother calls on a Monday and her voice sounds far away, as though she is shouting up from the bottom of a very deep hole.

Over the weekend, she explains, one of my brothers began using meth and pills again. He stopped for a while after one of our sisters tried to gouge his eyes out while she was high.

For months, this sister was picked up by the police for running into the ocean, or for walking barefoot along the highway while high on meth and cocaine. She crashed a car, ordered so many things on Amazon you could not walk into her home. She piled bags of garbage in her dining room. She overdosed, went to rehab. Overdosed, went to a psychiatric facility. She used for a year, for two. She would not stop, she said. A demon sat beckoning at the end of her bed, she said: she had begun to hallucinate him in her teens.

Her violence scared our brother sober for a time but now he is using again and he beat our youngest brother to a pulp before turning on our mother. When her son gets angry like this, my mother flits around to ensure his comfort. She flinches far too often. She forgives and sates his unquenchable thirst.

My mother called the cops. When they arrived, my brother said he would not stop. He talked to his reflection in the window. They took him away to a psychiatric facility.

Our youngest brother watched him carted away. He, too, uses daily, has been on probation for years, in and out of jail and psychiatric facilities twice in the last month. He went upstairs and cut his wrists. The cops came again. They took him away to a psychiatric facility.

Another sister learned about this and was reminded of her own cutting years ago, when she smoked and drank daily, spent long days in her dark bedroom. She still smokes every day but tries not to drink, though she sometimes does that too. She came the same day to drop her baby off at our parents' house before driving herself away to a psychiatric facility.

My mother loves her children. She tries to help, asking each and every one, "Baby, baby, what can I get you?"

I listen closely to my mother, buried so deep inside that hole. I try to make out the strata, the years layered on top of each other. The bones, too, from the creatures that could not escape.

�🜂

In Edvard Munch's oil painting *Self Portrait in Hell*, a slim figure stands nude in front of flame, staring directly at the artist. He is thin and vulnerable. The figure bears no detail on his body or arms, just a few on his face, dark eyes probing the viewer, a furrowed brow, lines etched across his forehead. The shading darkens near his head.

The real detail is in the background brushwork, a rhythmic swirl of light and shadow. In one corner a shadow looms. Does this shadow belong to the figure? The devil?

Perhaps it is both.

◊

I know something of this darkness. I recognize Blake's chaotic storm, have felt Fuseli's nightmare sitting on my chest. Sometimes when I drink, I gulp too greedily, hear my mother's too-quick laughter, her loud voice from my mouth, later staring at Munch's self-portrait in my bathroom mirror.

It wasn't always this way. I did not drink until nearly 21, then I carefully monitored the frequency after the college illusion that binge-drinking was safe wore away, once every few weeks, never alone, never when I was stressed or sad. I have never done drugs, never smoked a cigarette. Perhaps I am too prudish to try. Perhaps I am too afraid of what I've seen.

I do not drink often because the older I get, the more drinking feels like a dark homecoming. Merriment bleeds into misery. A sadness creeps in, the kind that feels as though I am being crushed by the weight of the world, sinking, sinking, hope a tiny pinprick of light so far away. In these moments, I try to climb up, but choke and sputter. In these moments, I cross a threshold where light gives way and my body knows in blood and bone: euphoric and terrible. I feel the certainty that if I were to keep going—tonight, tomorrow—that the descent would be both welcome and tragedy.

◊

His first day in the mine, the boy walks slowly, dragging his feet, kicking up dust. He turns around and looks back at the sky and sun. He hears birds trill their early morning call.

Over the sound of the men, their heavy boots, the clang of their picks, he can make out the canary in its cage, whistling in the dimming light, desperate to join the birds at the surface.

The boy holds his breath as long as he can, savoring that mix of fresh air and clover, last night's rain and the breakfast coffee. He walks deeper, deeper, the light and his breath giving out.

His lungs burn, like his eyes from the soot. The tunnel demands he cave, submit. He halves himself for his duty.

In the cage, the canary goes quiet.

CARVE

"She lived—as lived the violence of our years with him, knifed into us like scrimshaw cut in living bone. Carved but alive, we learned to hold our breath, dive deep, bare our teeth to what fed us."
— *Joy Castro*

Whale tooth the size of a palm held open for offerings, for help. Surface blade-slick, oiled with fat flayed and boiled. How your tooth shines when you are stripped of your flesh, rubbed down with your own disappearance.

Taste sea, salt and regret, seep of sex.

A ship is carved on your whale tooth, a dozen billowing masts, taut lines wrestling with the wind. You know those ropes, the ways they choke, capturing the body and holding it like an embrace.

The image was etched with a hundred pricks of a needle before the knife engraved a clean line, connecting so many dots into a picture. Scrimshaw is the art of etching onto bone, tooth or tusk, even cartilage, that material meant to soften the blow.

You know the pierce, the pain, the will of another carved into you, that story imposed on your own bone.

✿

Bruises mark dark stars on my hipbones, jutting angry at my jeans and the floor my cousin pins me down against. At ten, I flap my arms like a butterfly, but I cannot escape his knee on my back, his hands gripped tight around my wrists.

He is pale and breathless and smells sour as he greedily gulps the air. I cannot breathe, feel as though I am drowning in the dark room.

Later he releases me and I swim to the door, though not to the shore. His bones carve into mine—a story I never tell.

&

In the bathtub, I pretend to be a mermaid. My hair is long enough that my mother must help me wash it, though I am silent when the tangles hurt. Already I've learned that in exchange for legs—the ability to run—a girl must be quiet.

Instead, I wish myself to the sea. I imagine a star upon my heart. I hold my legs closed, tight, tight, toes turned out like in ballet class where we wear costumes silvery as fish, gliding through the air as though it were water.

With my tailfin, I am boneless. I am free. With my girlmouth I can say that only when I'm alone do I think I might be pretty and that my stomach hurts from holding things in and I like talking underwater because no one can hear but the bubbles remind me of the power of my breath.

When I am out of the bath and dry and my mother is brushing my hair, I watch the Disney story where a mermaid decides to give up her softness, the salt smell of her home, for the hollow of a human waist, her song lost underwater like a scream.

&

Crudity marks early 18th century scrimshaw. The craft was one of lurch and compromise, rough hands and bulky sailing needles hewing art from bone on a pitching ship.

An unskilled hand holds you. Listless, angry at the monotony of swell and surge, a medium he cannot control. He captures you, white whale, flays you ragged, strips you of your good meat to crush between his molars. He lays you out in strips to dry. Boils you down to glisten.

You are dismantled. You now exist in parts: crackling skin salted crisp, sweet meat to feed on, oil to light his way in the dark, perfume for his women when he returns to shore. Your ribs will corset girls in place so they, too, cannot swim away.

☼

I collect sand dollars with my grandmother because I do not know they are alive. I palm the smooth circle, a star pinpricked like a story across the surface. I believe an artist has left his hand until I find a dozen more with the same story across the sucking sand that pulls as if to drag my feet under. The picture, my mother's mother explains, is one of survival.

The creature is a tiny urchin, spines lining its body. It would pierce my flesh it if could, bleed me into the sand. The star shape I covet is a series of holes where the creature releases its tube feet to breathe, to scurry away.

A sand dollar likes to dig, like my grandmother and me, the way we burrow our feet into the beach. The sand dollar survives by burying itself, by living underground, out of sight. To endure, they must stand on their sides, perched as if on a brittle spine, must face the oncoming current to catch food in their open wailing mouths.

Living like the dead, half-buried and scuttling, allows them to survive longer than most in the stinking sea. Sand dollars can live up to ten years, or until a young girl palms their star picture, something pretty to put on her dresser at home.

The star image gets stronger, more vivid as the creature suffocates, starves in the brittle cage. Soon the shell is sharp enough I cut my finger, suck at the blood and do not know where I end and the creature begins, do not know the origins of the salt.

☼

The gentle arc of my ribs in college, the reassurance of counting my architecture. In my dorm room, my fingers rest in the soft vulnerabilities between bones.

My ribs press hard and hungry against the skin stretched during the year I will not eat. I understand bone as the cage of the body.

I feel my tail—ravenous and wild—bone on the floor, paining, pining me down as if I am an animal under glass.

My bones grow large as my body goes small, so small the blood stops, and I am all clavicle and elbow, all lank and limb, my hunger etched for all to see.

When I step into the sea as an adult, it is a different ocean than that of my childhood. An entire continent separates me now from my old home, and I live on a finger of land that curves into the water and back on itself as if pointing to the past or spiraling like a mollusk shell.

The salt smells different, the sand fine and white, rocks and creatures ground down over the millennia. I wander shores and visit museum galleries lined with the dead.

A narwhal's horn is a tooth inside out, reads a placard, millions of nerves exposed to the elements. The creature's heart rate changes when the tusk feels cold or heat, or with changes in salinity. The creature lives with its vulnerabilities on display, raw hurts pointing to the sky. It cannot hide.

It will not survive. Narwhals only grow two teeth in their lifetime, gumming their food despite their supposed ferocity, and most narwhal tusks are lost in the expanse. This rarity makes narwhals—like all creatures whose potential for pain is visible—something to hunt. They are endangered like the whale, the walrus, like the rising, warming sea.

A little boy pushes his sister out of the way, runs his hands over the tusk replica and says it would make a good sword. The girl looks down at her feet, nurses her hurt.

Most female narwhals lose their tusks, if they ever develop them at all, says the museum guide. Does the boy feel how soft the tusk is? Pliable to our will, bendable nearly a foot in either direction. It is not as strong as we think. It is perfect for carving into because the tusk hardens from the inside.

How to hide in the sea with your bones on display, your hurt exposed and inviting. How to survive when your weapon is a wanting.

I pass the gift shop on my way outside to the fog and bitter gulls, scrimshaw for sale in the windows, reflecting behind my mouth pressed firm like the horizon.

�™

One of my hipbones sits higher than the other, lurching forward an inch like it is trying to escape. This side of my body is clenched with a fear it can't forget, a marrow kind of knowing.

Pain snakes up, coils chronic around my neck. Behind my jaw it feels as though a knee is on my vertebrae.

I click when I talk, dolphin girl, bone and cartilage speaking a story to which no one listens.

☙

The scrimshander's rough hand worries a story across your smooth surface. His needles are carved of whale bone. He forces you to you injure yourself.

He whittles you away to pass his time. Pricks his story, a dozen stars, scars, into bone, all that is left of you. He drags a blade to make a constellation of your pain.

Snuffing the candle he made by boiling down your flesh, he soots your wounds for all to see.

☙

A man I knew in college used a knife to strip flesh from bone, blood seeping across his white countertop.

He separated tendon from tender meat, threw what he would not eat into a bucket for chum. Later he tossed it over the side of his boat, blood and bone seeing through water, drawing sharks to his side.

The mallet matched the pounding in my head. I watched him flatten the meat to see-through, as though he was sustained by the act of erasure.

I bled, too, from his violence. Flattened with the unrelenting weight of him until I was boneless, breathless, tender.

We burned my grandmother's body after she died. It blistered, blackened to smooth white bones before burning to a fine ash.

Her bones were thin as a bird's, though she never flew away—lived forty years with a man who used her bones to break his rage. They looked like the tiny pins that held up hair, captured it into a net, trapped it firmly in place.

As a child, I dug for bones in my backyard. A chicken wing or steak bone gnawed by a dog that was not mine. Tossed out scraps.

I tried to piece together the stories, to fit bone to bone to resurrect what had been broken.

Once I found a whole wishbone and—as if by instinct—snapped it with satisfaction.

The beast opens its mouth and the scrimshander witnesses a harp, wishing to run his fingertips, long gone rough and ragged from the ropes and the cold, across those sturdy strings, calling back the lullaby of his childhood to echo there in the cavernous mouth.

But today he selects his prey, watches the unsuspecting whale undulate, rising with the waves while men must fight the current. He cannot fathom accepting powerlessness.

He aims a harpoon; his pulse quickens at the pierce.

He likes the way the whale cries, so different from the gentle song that haunts him while he sleeps, calls him out of dreams to the deck, the ice and the wind making him brittle, carrying him further away.

He likes the way the blood comes. He likes the seep before the spurt, the pulse of that pain.

The hull heaves with the thrashing, gnashing weight of the whale. He smiles, witnessing a body wear down to nothing.

Later, he hoists the dead, shining with the sweat of what he's accomplished. He forces open the mouth, claims the largest tooth. He feeds himself, his art, on this theft.

When the boy tagged me on the elementary playground, pressing his palm hard into my back, I went down on the blacktop. I skinned my hands, looked up at him from bloodied knees.

Could he sign my cast? he later asked. He scrawled "You're it" in dark pencil, which sooted across the bright white.

The cast smelled of skin and sweat, sharp with salt. I danced *Swan Lake* with a broken wing and everyone laughed at a broken girl trying to be beautiful.

When the doctor sawed the cast off, my arm had withered to nothing. I learned how quickly the body gives up on itself.

My sister buoys boneless like the beluga beside her. She does not eat, like me, both of us retreating into the shells of ourselves, brittle homes strapped to our backs.

We have been watching our grandmother drown in morphine, her body swimming in the sheets of her hospital bed. She is bone and sinew, doctors say, the weight of her skeleton heavy against her skin, purple bruise tidepooling across her limbs.

They have tied her down, arms, legs, and head, so she will not grab at the tube they have inserted into her throat. She looks like a star splayed. She looks like a fish gasping for breath.

I hold my grandmother's hand, her hurt in mine. I stack our bones.

My sister cannot bear to come to the hospital, so afraid is she of death, of the hurt that has begun to pool around her lately, the tide that she can't seem to swim against.

We go to Sea World to escape the white hospital walls, the way they press in, the way the fluorescent lights make looking up like peering from under water. My sister will swim with the dolphins, will descend into her fear and emerge triumphant.

But she is tearful, fearful of the cold and the camera. She looks as though she can't breathe, and through the slick wetsuit I can see her hipbones jutting, each vertebra like a mollusk down her spine. They match my own.

She rejects the dolphin with its frantic smile, the way it seeks approval with such desperation. She will not accept love so freely, without sacrifice. Instead, she prefers the beluga, the white undulation, the bulbous head she reaches for timidly.

The beluga is broken, accepting touch without consent. With her pale skin and hair, my sister matches the dispirited creature—they both look like ghosts.

When they descend, I stand with my back against a cage, smelling rotting fish and flesh. I hear a noise, something guttural and starved. I turn to see a walrus with a broken tusk and cloudy eyes. He follows me by hearing, his thick whiskers following my palm, desire on display. I cannot bear the pitiful way he snorts, the way his bone curves out as if to caress.

I wonder what the whale hears above water, below. Can it hear my sister's body seizing up, the fear she carries in her limbs like me, like our grandmother? We each hear the world in echo.

The beluga has no bones in its head, empty, hollow. How, too, I wish to be boneless.

"Smile," we say to my sister who is alternating between thrashing to stay afloat and weeping into the waves. She opens her mouth to show her teeth like a cage.

✺

The morning my grandmother dies, my razor slips in the shower and I peel away a strip of skin from my ankle, the hurt taking me closer to the bone.

Injury is intimate, and I feel the knot in my neck, my crooked hip, realize the way her broken bones grew back twisted, her fingers pointed as if to run away, clavicle knotted at her throat. I recognize her crooked gait as my own.

Crouching low in the shower, I finger my grief, my careless wound already beginning to scar. Bloody water disappears down the drain.

✺

Conus hieroglyphus is small as a thumb broken at the knuckle, chestnut and cream. The story of the shell is marked on its surface, runes like danger or help.

The shell tells its own tale, does not rely on another to etch the narrative. The sea and the stones do not mark the pictures, nor an artist's tool. The shell's stories are a warning.

Touch the hieroglyphics and hurt. The snails inside are predatory, venomous. They will sting your flesh, leave their mark across your palm.

The shell wears omen like a necklace, the jewelry made from other conus creatures, the puka I wore as a child, the dead dangling from my throat.

◊

In college a man stalked me through spring and summer, broke into my home, pinned me down, left his handprints across my body. I did not wear a bathing suit to the beach those seasons, my spine lined with bruises from being perched too long on the sharp edge of fear.

He held his hand over my mouth when I screamed, said no, smiled too much or not enough. His hands tasted like the ocean we lived near and the expensive leather of his steering wheel and the slick sheen of power. And it tasted like me, a strange fearful animal, salt and sex, something sacred turned scared smeared across my face.

One day I talked too fast, my hands darting because a body that has learned to panic and the bones that remember the stones thrown at a midnight window, a man smirking outside, mouthing, "Let me in or I will hurt you" are skittish. My palms flew up for an offering, for help—waving "Save me, I'm drowning here in the ocean of him"— hoping anyone might send aid, though no one ever did.

By accident or instinct, my finger went up his nose, hit bone. For once, I ricocheted inside of him, left him bruised and bleeding. And for a moment, as he let go his grip of my leg, which kept me close to him when I wanted to run, I learned what it means to leave your mark on bone.

◊

Tusk and tooth are fragile. They discolor, dry out. They warp without the protection of a mouth.

To preserve scrimshaw, scrimshanders submerge their art in the dark of a barrel. They leave you in the oil of your own boiled body to drown.

&

I oil my scars to soften them. The droplet of scalding water that leapt from the pot to my cheek like a tear. The chicken pox on my eyelid.

Two fingernails another dragged across my arm to watch me bleed. The angry purple places left when my immune system retaliated against hidden hurts, brought forth a hundred bleeding vessels, scabs rising like the dead.

The ankle reminder from the morning my grandmother died.

My widening hips leaving stretchmark lattice like a net.

&

A ship is carved on your whale tooth, a dozen billowing masts, taut lines wrestling with the wind. You know those ropes, the ways they choke, capturing the body and holding it like an embrace.

Look close. At the root of the tooth a whale curves like a question. See the way you coil in the ragged sea. See your beast back arched, tail lashing in the sky. See how you dive, headfirst back home.

Do not crack to the marrow, do not let another steal that yellow glisten. When they slick you with oil, be sure it is enough so you cannot be held down.

MOON CALL

In the velvet gloaming, I can barely make out the figures gathered, plates of BBQ on their laps, glasses of thick tea to wash sauce from our smiles. We are featureless, shadowy suggestions.

Our host sets up a screen, taut against the soft New England night, illuminating it with a bright spotlight. He is a ghostly silhouette behind the screen, the dark summer woods creeping close. The daylight has been fading for hours, a slow August decline that makes the sun seem a suitor, the moon a stranger. Now, the spotlight is a makeshift moon hovering low in the yard. We squint, but as if by instinct our eyes are drawn to the false celestial.

Weekends camping with my parents by the California shore, I collected driftwood and dry leaves to toss into the nightly flame. I waited for the moon to appear above the ocean horizon, blue stretching into blue so far and wide it made me feel small and dizzy. Fascinated by the moon as a child, I could not look away. The orb seemed a welcoming, the craters a call.

We camped near the shore, the smell of salt and brine, the gentle lapping of the water. The sand was fine and swallowed my feet if I was not careful. When I walked to where the water enveloped the land, waves creeping higher and higher to frighten me, then retreating as if to imply I'd imagined the fear, my footprints vanished quickly, as if to say I did not matter, had never existed.

Near the campsite was a monarch grove where each winter, tens of thousands of butterflies migrated to cluster together for warmth. The eucalyptus trees dripped with orange, the limbs alive with wing, opening and closing as the creatures vibrated heat. They nestled as one, drawn to this place each season as if by intuition. When I looked up into their beating bodies, it felt like seeing my heart.

As the night swelled around us, the ocean became a suggestion, the mist overtaking our campsite clearing, my hand in front of my face vanishing if I reached too far forward or ventured too far from our makeshift fire. If you were not careful, I realized, the darkness would simply swallow you up.

Only when I looked up could I find the light, find my way home.

🔥

Surrounded by the charcoal grill smoke, we readjust our eyes to the spotlight. After a few moments, the moths arrive, dotting the screen like rain. They cannot help but fall for our host's fluorescent moon.

The cabbage moth looks celestial, greenish-white, as though illuminated from inside, dark spots cratering wings. The harnessed tiger moth's wing topography is black and white, but when it shifts, I spy an orange body beneath, believing it, for a moment, to be the monarch of my childhood.

Back in California, the monarchs are declining. The western butterflies lost 97% of their population during my childhood from the 1980s to mid-2010s. In the winter of 2018-2019, the monarch population declined by 86% in a single year, a decrease of more than 99% since the 1980s. Now, less than thirty thousand monarchs dot the skies with color. In winter, the eucalyptus trees are barren rather than beating.

My adopted grandmother, a lifelong family friend, says she cannot plant flowers anymore because the California drought has left the land ravaged. The fox that once lived in her backyard is gone, and the squirrels too. Even the birds have left, she mourns, lonely for their sound, leaving plates of water out for them, though the water evaporates in the blistering sun.

"There was once a town in the heart of America," wrote Rachel

88

Carson, "where all life seemed to live in harmony with its surroundings. Then a strange blight crept over the area and everything began to change. There was a strange stillness. The few birds seen anywhere were moribund; they trembled violently and could not fly. It was a spring without voices. On the mornings that had once throbbed with the dawn chorus of scores of bird voices there was now no sound; only silence lay over the fields and woods and marsh." Her 1962 book *Silent Spring* is an environment call to action whose warnings about the dangers of pesticides and natural degradation is eerily familiar, though its focus on DDT allows many to write the book off as outdated.

My adopted grandmother recalls her grandfather's own sod house, the cool damp provided by living in the belly of the earth. The soil found its way into the print of her foot, and though she indented the soil when she walked, her steps also returned the land to itself.

And she recalls running behind the family tractor while the DDT billowed in great clouds all around, left what looked like rain on her skin. She danced in the mist, ran through the chemical clouds, the whole world ethereal, otherworldly.

Now she does not recognize her home or her aging reflection in the window when she looks outside. The fields are dead or on fire, California burning each year, smoke clotting out the sky, black clouds raining down ash, never water.

Meanwhile, in Massachusetts, the rain comes too often and it feels like drowning. It is too cold for butterflies to winter here, too icy and bleak.

It is late summer and already we need fire to keep us warm. My host places log after log, stoking the flame for his guests. In a few weeks, the moths that dot the screen in front of me will die.

This is why so many cluster and cling to the illuminated screen. Our host points out each one. They are delicate and furred, soft-bodied and warm. Their wings are bold with color or softly pastel. The wings sharp edges, or curved like lace. They are soft as a whisper, a lover's hand, foam gathered at the ocean lip.

Many, like the winter moth and large heath, feature elaborate camouflage, so intent they are to escape from view. In this moment, however, they are willing to compromise exposure. They are desperate for the light.

◊

In college I was lonely and I was cold. I flitted from one warm body to the next, looking for someone that felt like home.

One night, I gathered to stargaze around a campfire next to a lover who would leave me. It was dark and he was distant. I moved closer to the fire, the way I had as a child, the faces around me becoming many in shadow. Multiple and shapeshifting. I wondered if I would recognize myself in that light.

When my shoes caught fire, I did not realize. But there I was, my footprints turned to flame, the smell of melting rubber. After I stamped the fire out, the tread marks vanished.

Later, I wandered into the woods to find the restroom. As I tried to return to the fire, I realized my shoes no longer left a print. The moon had disappeared behind the clouds and I struggled to find my path.

◊

Our host tells the story of when he protected butterflies in a former military training area. Most of the bombs had been removed, so the warnings said, but no one was certain.

The land was transformed into an insect sanctuary, because insect populations on land are declining at nearly 1% a year, some studies suggesting as much as 2.5% annually. A 2019 review indicated that 40% of insect species could become extinct in the next few decades.

All day he looked from the ground to the sky, he explains, careful of his foot on the land, the creatures in his hand. He captured and released butterflies and moths, hoping they would overtake the surrounding area.

The field was filled with flowers—tall phlox and black-eyed Susans, Indian grass and bright bee balm. Purple coneflower mixed with Virginia bluebell, and blue wild indigo, and beardtongue, and turtlehead, and bugbane, all drifting in the breeze. The fragrance of marsh blazing star, wild bergamot, goldenrod, slender mountain mint, and white wood aster lingered on his clothes long after he left. Butterflies and bees flitted between blooms, pollen sticky thick on their bodies.

At night, moths and bats pollinated, bright with moonlight.

His face is ghostly with light as he tells this story—blooms and bombs buried, only a matter of time before either burst.

◊

I didn't like the fury of moths gathering at camp lights, porch lights, and street lights as a child. They frightened me. The way their bodies flurried and pulsed.

It is speculated that moths are drawn to light because they evolved for many years with only the moon as their evening light source. The moonlight led them to blossom and sweet, to protection and heat. When monarchs traveled three thousand miles each winter, the moonlight led them home.

Later, as humans harnessed firepower, the blazing light began to lead moths astray. But the moon in its ever-fixed position, waxing and waning through 190 million years, always called them back.

Now we draw moths with our many lights, confusing them from their pollinating purpose, which is believed to be larger and more complex than daytime pollinators like bees. Store lights, fluorescent signs, and spot-lit billboards compel and distract moths, preventing flowers from flourishing.

As a child, I could not decide if I felt jealous of the moths' fervor or sick for the trick, the sound of moths hitting the camping lanterns, as though they would break either it or themselves to have at the light, the warmth, the way they were fooled, beckoned to their death.

The adults, meanwhile, didn't appreciate the moths, swatting them away from campfires and candlelit tables, lighting citronella and spraying harsh chemicals, the foggy night air thick with the smell.

The sound of moth bodies brittled at the electric zapper, the sparks of their deaths raining down on the campsite like Fourth of July fireworks. They were compelled and frantic, the way I feel now as an adult when I am unmoored, pulled to the glow of a screen—telephone, television, the fake sun each morning and fake fireplace each winter evening.

When the winter seems as if it will never thaw, I watch nature documentaries where the world is green and thrumming with life. I watch birds of paradise unfurl brilliant plumage, foxes fly through the air, jeweled frogs as small as my thumbnail. I watch all the creatures I could never imagine into being and by the time the show is complete, so too is another species extinct.

As soon as it is spring, I go outside to my Massachusetts woods where groundhogs feast on clover and the wild turkey nests in a pile of hay. A mother deer brings her two unsteady fawns through the yard on their spindly legs. Red foxes and coyotes venture from the woods onto the grass to play. A red-tailed hawk dips into the meadow for crickets and mice. Great blue herons loop through the sky before landing in the woods to nest.

Dragonflies appear in summer, metallic green and electric blue, darting about the yard, landing nearby as I garden, creeping closer, curious. Bees feast on clover while wasps construct a papier-mâché nest beneath the eaves of the house. Everywhere, butterflies in sun. At night the sky is teeming with mosquitos and moths and the bats that loop lazily to gather their fill. When I look to the moon, the sky is alive.

Next door, my neighbor dumps insecticides into the protected wetlands, urges me to do the same to keep our BBQs pest-free, to keep the wasps away from his daughter. Every month, a company comes to spray insecticides over his property, where they mist in the air, glint on the grass before soaking into soil, the well-water beneath.

After, I taste metal in the air.

◊

It is cold away from the fire, but our host is fascinating and our many bodies, bustling together as we watch the moths, generate enough heat to keep us warm.

The morning cloak is deep garnet-dotted teal and edged in yellow. The cloudless sulphur beats wings of mantis-green. The common checkered skipper is downy soft as a mouse.

One moth comes from Montana. One moth lives for seven months, another for eleven. One moth looks like a Zabulon skipper except for its mottled wing pattern.

Our host knows each one, recalling from memory how they pupate and pulse. Looking up in the sky he recognizes the flight patterns of the ash sphinx and great oak dagger. He calls out each name.

◊

In school we collected insects for a grade. We were to trap them any way we could, points awarded for biodiversity and the careful way we stuck each creature through with a pin.

Everyone had a roly poly, the ones whose abdomens split to reveal a hundred squirming babies if you bent them backwards enough to break. And grasshoppers and pincher bugs and black pinacate stinkbugs that sent the class outdoors with their sulphureous odor. And everyone had monarchs, of course, because we were young and they were plenty.

But a praying mantis was rare, the stoic calm and soft curved hands. So too a hawkmoth, though we had all seen the bright green hornworms hanging from tomato plants. Somebody found a tarantula, which we'd all seen, but only one was brave enough to pierce with a pin, watch it scramble to nowhere.

But the best prize went to the child who found a Jerusalem cricket, big as a thumb, waxy and flightless, oozing through the cardboard display long after its death.

Education, we were taught, was calling creatures forward to their capture. We sat beneath our porch lights, listening to the buzz and captured moths in the tiny nets the teacher provided; we caught fireflies in jars on summer vacations to the Midwest and East Coast, decapitating them and smearing the fluorescence across our arms like magic. We watched sea monkeys and ants in their farms until we were too bored to care for them any longer and let them dry and die. We captured caterpillars in jars, watched them build chrysalises in that glass imprisonment, rebirth anew, our hands ready to reach inside to rub their wings without realizing this rendered them flightless.

In the butterfly and moth habitat at the zoo, we felt the sun heating up the glass, the air confined and claustrophobic. We were told not to touch the creatures but they landed on us anyway, a contact so light many of us crushed them in fright before the class was sent outside for a lecture on the sanctity of natural life.

Later, in the gift store, we saw a dozen brilliant butterflies pressed flat behind glass, ours to keep forever, for a price.

◊

Once the moon is high in the sky, drifting in and out of the cloud cover, our host turns off the light. One by one, the moths drift away, leaving us as quickly as they came.

Suddenly it is only us and the dark, and one by one folks pull out their phones, drawn to the artificial light. It is time to go, and they pull up the digital maps that will lead them on the winding ways home. They leave, illuminated by their screens in their cars, their headlights piercing.

When the moon is swallowed, I cannot see. I look to where the light once was, but our host is folding away the screen, his back turned to face the woods, the wildness creeping closer.

ON REFLECTION

I can recall the moment I realized the girl staring back at me in the mirror was already past, that the reality reflected in the glass was of a time already gone.

As a child I retreated to the restroom to read when I should have been getting ready for bed, the room full of echoes: the steady faucet drip, the gentle ring of bubble bath around the tub, my parents murmuring from the living room. Climbing to the sink, I would seek myself in the mirror above the counter.

One evening when I was five or six, my reflection became a question. I knew it was me, but the longer I stared, the more fully my image became a stranger.

The odd feeling that I existed both in and out of that reflection was unsettling, for neither was fully real. She was girl and ghost, and the contradiction of duality weighed heavy in my stomach as I began to float. I could not tell where or when or even if I began.

Holding my face close to the mirror, I studied the image closely, so convinced it could not be me at the same time I knew it to be true, that I scarcely noticed that my breath fogged the glass, barely heard my mother from the other room calling me back.

������☾

Created in 1970 by American psychologist Gordon Gallup Jr., the mirror test is designed to determine whether an animal is capable of self-recognition. The test is simple—animals are anesthetized and marked with a spot of red paint or a sticker on a part of their body they can't normally see. When they wake, they are placed in front of a mirror. If the animal investigates the new mark, they are considered capable of self-awareness.

Most animals fail the test. Only humans, a few apes, a single Asiatic elephant, dolphins, orcas, the Eurasian magpie, and cleaner wrasse fish have passed—and scientists disagree on the majority of these successes. Most animals simply gaze in the mirror.

Humans don't pass the test until they are toddlers, and this often occurs after extensive coaxing where the toddlers learn to mirror the adults around them. Recently, rhesus monkeys and small fish have learned to pass the test, indicating that they are latently aware of the self, or, at the very least, capable of learning new cognitive skills.

For many years, it was assumed that animals who passed the test were capable of reflecting on their being and identity, and, by extension, potentially understanding that other animals have distinct selves and minds. But this is assumption, abstraction based on what we observe when watching animals watch themselves.

In 2011, photographer James Geddes captured the image of an eagle standing on frozen ice, staring down at its reflection. The photo seems quintessentially American—the symbol of freedom pensive at its likeness, a national self-reflection captured a few years after Obama took office and began to write a narrative of hope and the country responded by beginning to unravel.

The eagle's reflection is crisp and sharp, the bird craning its neck forward to peer closer. It is easy to read the image as one of contemplation: the eagle considering its place in a changing world, assessing the apparent stability of ground even as the water rushes underneath.

⟁

The world is always leaving.

I realized this young. My body was a vehicle, time a stretch of road. There was no choice but to move forward, try to stay in the careful lines to avoid a collision. If I did stray, the car would rumble, the road designed to keep me in, to startle me back in position if I tried to leave or simply drifted unaware.

From my position in the passenger seat, I witnessed how the reality of the road in front of me could become a memory fading behind. We were always heading to the future, even if the destination was a museum that celebrated the past: polished silver cups or obsidian knives glinting under the lights, my gape-mouthed reflection in the glass. The beach was full of waves retreating forward and back, and I tried to capture that blurring sense of time on my tiny camera, though mostly I strained my eye to find the mirror inside. I tried to capture my kitten growing bigger each day, the way the window reflected sunlight on my lap, rainbows through the air, my own face looking in a mirror so I could see both versions of myself at once.

Objects in mirror are closer than they appear, read the rear-view mirror. I did not understand, for perceptions of depth and time have always made me dizzy. I like the unreality of compressing time, past and present not so different, or looking down from a tall building, stomach drooping into my temple.

Caution, my parents explained. It meant that when you've left something behind it can sneak up on you, that you are never as far ahead of something as you believe. That the narrative of your present is crafted by the past.

Invented in 1903, the two-way mirror is not a mirror of binaries, of doubles. The mirror is actually referred to as a *one-way*, the name a trick, much like the device.

A mirror is made by applying a thick layer of reflective material to the back of a sheet of glass in order to make it opaque. When we gaze into the mirror, the layer of silvering reflects our image back at us. In a one-way mirror, however, the silvering is applied by half, so that the glass is not opaque, but translucent, ethereal. Half the light striking the glass passes through it, the other half reflects.

This mirror is often used to mislead, to interrogate. Those gazing at the mirror from a brightly-lit room see themselves reflected, while those on the other side in a room dimly-lit are obscured. The mirror is deception, a play of light and shadow, expectation and ego.

Turn the lighting up on both sides and the reflection disappears, the mirror simply glass, images free to float between the veil.

◊

At the start of 2020, I have not looked into a mirror for over four years. I do not know when my childhood fascination with the self—the certainty of its mutability—shifted into grief. I only know that at some point I grew wary of the reflection, not my likeness but my living.

The last time I can recall looking into the mirror without dread was when the world was on the cusp of dismantling. There was a new president, a new climate, a new decade approaching, time gone fast and slow all at once. Trump took office as I reluctantly claimed a new job and thus a new home, neither of which I wanted, though I knew I was lucky.

In my early twenties I'd watched eagerly as California faded from the rear-view mirror, a new home in Nebraska on the horizon, but nearly a decade later as Nebraska faded from sight and Massachusetts came into focus, I felt only disappointment. The life, the home, the country were nothing like I'd expected, nothing I'd written for myself.

Within days of arriving, I caught sight of my face in the mirror, saw my mouth pinched into a straight line like the horizon behind me, eyes glazed like a museum specimen frozen in the past. The image was a ghost of who I had been before, and for months I stood before her, tried to fake-smile at the me in the mirror the way I did with people at work, though there was no one I wanted to smile at, or at strangers in the street, though Massachusetts seemed full of resentments bitter as the cold and I missed the quiet comfort of Nebraska and the golden beaches of my California youth.

Soon I was haunting my own life, caught in the present while longing for the past. I was nostalgic for my father's classic rock buzzing through the radio while we dipped low into a backroad, or peeling the skin of a California acorn to reveal the mealy flesh beneath. I missed the way the ocean wind made me forget precision, hair whipping in my mouth, nose running, and the way the summer heat pooled in the parts of my body I would otherwise forget, mingling with the smell of sunscreen and BBQ. I wanted the messy freedom of my girlhood, where time stretched long into the afternoon and abandoned walls were for bouncing balls against, rocks for gathering heavy in your pocket and flinging from high vistas or across a still lake. I missed the promise of a few years past, sipping wine with friends late into the night, knowing I might never see them again, which was what made our stories more compelling long after the candles had spilled their wax across the table to pool like amorphous phantoms.

I was nostalgic for the environment of my childhood too, the country a place that grew more fractured. I didn't recognize the images of my country just as I didn't recognize the images of myself. The television showed children in cages and women crying for their lost families, soldiers on the Capitol steps and Nazi flags. The news reported storms ravaging the coastlines, leaving countries in the dark, washing away cities, tornadoes snaking through the South, hurricanes hovering over the East, the West Coast black and burning each year. Online, friends and family argued over two seemingly-different worlds, each inhabiting their own side of the mirror, unable or unwilling to turn on the light to see the other. It was as though the image of the world and those within it had been smashed, the country's reflection reduced to jagged shards.

What was reality and what was perception melted before me, politicians reporting everything was fine just as I reported the same to those who asked how I was doing, though I could no longer look in the mirror without weeping or seizing up in panic. Once, I caught sight of myself in a restaurant mirror and lost my appetite, so sad I was for that lonely, lost woman.

It was unsettling to see the images of my reality reflected back at me—a country that seemed to be, like the climate itself, on the verge of extinction, each home I'd known under attack, fires threatening to burn my childhood California to rubble, tornadoes winding themselves like a noose around Nebraska, snow threatening to bury Massachusetts, leaving us as dark and dead as I felt most days. The forward momentum of my childhood proved incorrect—I'd driven forward, but now there was nowhere else to go, only ocean at this other end of the continent. And the danger in the rearview mirror was much closer than it appeared. So I simply stopped looking.

To be clear, I didn't disdain my appearance as much as mourn for the woman trapped as if behind glass in a place and position she never wanted to claim. Though I loved my childhood in the golden light of small-town California, from my vantage point many miles and years away, I realized it had written a narrative of sameness on me—one that defined my gender, sexuality, and speaking in a way that sought to silence. Though I loved my husband, our marriage after nearly a decade seemed stifling and prescriptive and felt, the longer I was in the role of wife, like it was closing in all around. Though I loved my work, I took a job I did not particularly want because there are few in my field and we are told to be grateful, and after I arrived, the photo filters were removed one by one until all that remained was the grainy image of my new reality. I'd sought movement for many years, thrilled by the images whirring out the window, my face reflected over them in the glass, but I realized now it was the other way around, that my image was the one upon which the world had been superimposed.

The longer time went on, the more blurred and faint the image of myself, my home, my country seemed. Everything felt lost, disappeared by a power beyond our control. It pained me to see what I had become without my permission so I simply stopped looking at myself at all, stopped taking photos so as not to mark this passage of time.

I spent so much time longing for the past that at a certain point I felt nearly dead, as though I were a ghost haunting my own life. Nostalgia and haunting are not so very different, after all—we are only nostalgic for things that are gone, we are only haunted by the things we once loved.

◊

I used to read beside my reflection, my child body curled up with a book on the bathroom counter. Mirrors seemed to be everywhere— the bathroom, the car, the vanity in my bedroom, the walls of ballet class where we were told to be strong but also small enough to disappear. They were in the glint of a knife and the windows of buildings where I saw myself pulled forward by the hand, my feet moving by duty rather than desire. The city skylines of every place I visited were lined with mirrors as if to reflect the world back onto itself, but the older I got, the more I saw confusion, the way a mirror faced against a mirror created reflections to infinity, no sense of logic or place. The way a bird flew into a window believing it sky.

I read books about ghosts because, like time or gravity or the certainty that my body would remember to breathe or beat, it filled me with wonder and a bit of fright. I read the one where a boy finds a mirror in the attic that can make him invisible. He likes disappearing and makes a little game of it, the way I liked to look at myself in the mirror to be both image and abstraction. Eventually the boy disappears for too long, struggling to find his way home.

I thought about how one day my angry grandfather was alive and then he was dead and my grandmother seemed like she could finally breathe. I thought about how my friend down the road with the best climbing trees moved away and then her trees were forbidden even though I knew all the footholds and how to reach one hand around the branch to the knot at the back, hoisting myself up and into the pine, sap glistening across my thighs as I looked across the riverbed to my house on the other side, the river disappearing, the bed full of cracks where the water vanished, birds pecking at the dry ground. I thought about how every spring the eucalyptus groves where the monarchs wintered were emptied and the flutter of gold vanished and though this was the way it should be, it was hard not to wonder if the butterflies would ever return. And I thought about how the historic mission in my town had stood for centuries but then it rained too much and the wall around the graveyard—the one my parents said kept the spirits in—collapsed and what would keep them in now or would they wander lonely through the town, confused why it seemed familiar though everything was different?

There is a delay between seeing and perceiving. It takes our brains a moment to process what we are looking at, so the image of my girlhood I saw in the mirror was from the past. At the mirror, I was both there and then. I was present and past, living and memory, girl and ghost. The longer I thought about time, how fast it goes—the first reflection I saw in the mirror long gone just as the one I was currently seeing was suspect, a version of myself I could no longer get back— the more I felt the sad sweet swell of nostalgia. I was only five, then six, then eight and ten, twenty and thirty, but already I was longing for and missing what was right in front of me.

One of my favorite books told the story of a young girl named Jane who visits her family in New England one summer and becomes intrigued by a garden reflecting ball. She spends long hours gazing at the reflection in the mirrors, the way they refract reality, until she begins, like me when I look in the mirror for too long, to see things that aren't real.

Then, one day, Jane sees the ghost of a wicked girl named Emily. She does not know where one girl ends and the other begins, what is present and what is past. The adults around her say it's make-believe like my parents say when they pull me away from the mirror to play in the real world. Jane and Emily merge into one.

I read the book time and again for a fright, stopping to stare at my reflection like a moon in the darkness of my bedroom window or in the skylight high in the bathroom ceiling, my pale face looking up as if from the end of a long tunnel.

◊

It is myth that a mirror inverts your image. You do not reflect in reverse. Instead, the left of your face is imposed on the left of the mirror, the right over the right. It is merely illusion—another trick of perception—that you exist altered. This is why photos and videos of ourselves seem so unnatural. We are more used to existing in the lag time between reflection and perception.

To view an accurate image, you must position two mirrors together at ninety degrees, stand at the split, straddle the images on either side. You must exist in multiples, view yourself from where the many selves join.

A true mirror is one that projects your image as others see you. Wave your right hand and the three-dimensional image will wave as if from the left. Lean to one side and see yourself lean away. The image is lifelike in a way that a traditional mirror is not and the experience disrupts our understanding of reflection, at once more human and intimate than our many years brushing our teeth or hair at the abstraction in front of us.

Some are startled, shaken, some shamed they have understood themselves incorrectly. And some weep at the rare chance to witness the self in as it truly exists in time and space.

◊

Now, in my mid-thirties, I am trying to see myself as I exist rather than as I reflect. I am searching for the place where the two mirrors come together to reveal the truth.

The image of the woman and the world I have been avoiding is both reflection and abstraction, the images not quite accurate, but ones I have been mourning these past few years. I have been so distracted by perceived loss that I've missed things disappearing right before me, even my own sense of wonder.

I no longer want to hang a Victorian veil over the mirror as though I am dead, as though the looking glass might trap my soul, prevent me from moving on. I want to go back to that girl in the mirror, watching, searching, enthralled by the many versions of the self.

When I stare in the mirror now, as I am (re)learning to do, as our reliance on video chats requires these months and years we isolate, the woman before seems a stranger and a support. I marvel at the way memory and nostalgia compress time so that I am here and then, in mirror and memory, the me of now and also of a split second ago and also all those years ago when I first stared in the mirror, headband pushing hair from my face, teeth starting to jut through the gums, that slow smile of recognition.

Reflection is both the mirrored image and careful rumination. I've been avoiding the image because I've been avoiding the thinking—about the homes I've made and the ways they do not fit, about the country changing underfoot. But these images I've avoided are not true reflections, and each is already gone. The only thing to do is remember there is no mirror test to convince your restless animal self that existence is precious, to convince you to step away from the reflection and into reality.

This doesn't mean we forget history or stop aching for it, mourning it if we must, but rather that living requires we keep some distance between our past and present, we keep our many selves in sight in the rearview mirror, as we determine which path to take and where to deviate.

♦

The first images of Earth were captured in the 1940s, a 35mm camera snapping a shot each second from a rocket, the photos falling back to land in a steel canister. What was reflected was revolutionary—horizon curve backdropped by space—but scientists worried over whether or not to release the images.

Earth surrounded by the vast dark of space, they feared, would counter people's self-perceptions. They thought people would feel insignificant, alone, fearful. They thought people might see human life as futile when faced with the vast isolation of space.

These first images fell to Earth from the future, but revealed a world already in the past. It is difficult to look at these photos without the complexity of time tugging comprehension in multiple directions. This image of the world is foreign and familiar, comfort and chaos. Astronauts tasked with leaving in order to move humankind forward to the edge of the galaxy, to live where the darkness was so deep there was no light to reflect, were compelled to turn back, nostalgic for what they'd abandoned.

RISING TIDE

My student overdoses the morning I learn my sister has been using. My student dies. My sister will overdose, later, but she will survive.

I am bleary-eyed in the sleet of a New England January morning. It's the kind of day that reminds me why the animals retreat underground, wait out half the year, will themselves dull and gaunt rather than search for growth in the desolate landscape. Each fall, the leaves go brilliant and draw tourists to these small towns, but they are an immolation, a surrender.

This place resonates hurts and haunts—the Puritan desire for reform echoing over stolen land, a landscape made by filling in the Boston Bay and paving over the garbage, the birth of a nation feeding itself on lobster and crab hoisted from the belly of the sea, feasting on the stink of those creatures, desperate and scuttling.

When I drive to campus, the small town gridlocks to circle around the awkward public square like a drain. In the rain, which is relentless this time of year, I wonder when I will simply wash away.

The square is oddly shaped and uneven. It's impossible for traffic to flow. It is, legend goes, the shape believed by the town's 1656 inhabitants to resemble Noah's Ark. The town will not remove this historical vestige, a reminder that the world was wicked, was banished inside during a flood to wait for forgiveness.

The university's announcement about my student's death, and emails from others in class who know—like I do—that she has likely overdosed, fill my inbox. She wrote about the drugs she used for twenty years, the way she felt like she couldn't breathe, was drowning unless she was high. How to critique a narrative like that, the steady march towards death?

I stare at my phone in the parking lot, hunched and cold in the early morning dark, the screen illuminated with loss. My student is dead and the campus trees seem dead, like those in the forest surrounding the house I recently bought with my husband who says we will have a white fence but not a child. At night, the woods echo with the sounds of predation and defeat.

And then my mother calls, her voice echoing across the line from California, where it is still night and raining. She says my sister is using. We wonder what can be done with a narrative like that as we each sit in our dark and watch the rising water.

The narwhal horn is frozen in shellac, resting beside the giant bluefin tuna and a great white shark, dead-eyed, mouth open in an eternal howl. Placards explain to museum visitors that the narwhal is real, a whale with a magical tusk that is actually a protruding canine tooth, the same kind of tooth we use to tear flesh. The creature is nearly extinct, due to hunting, another result of human failure to recognize our likeness.

Around the corner are a hundred animals shot on grand hunting expeditions a hundred years ago and stuffed for show. Despite the museum's restoration efforts, their fur is matted and the seams show. Tigers and bears are frozen into implausible poses like a curation of living death.

I struggle to find anything to say to my husband on this holiday of love, as other people's children pool all around our feet, taking in the carcasses.

We walk the corridor of evolution, time transforming dinosaurs into fish, reducing everything to extinction or smallness. Disappearance is the reward for survival.

My sister runs into the sea at midnight because her brain is on fire, her body is on fire, the world is on fire. She runs into the Pacific, hands up as if to fly because she wants to feel surrender.

The cops find her soaking and numb. She is not thirsty, she says. She will never stop using. The seals bark dissent. She announces her dog is her medical proxy. She has ordered a thousand dollars' worth of children's books she will never read to the children she does not have. The unopened boxes make a maze inside her tiny home. Trash lines the counters, maggots in the fridge.

When she was a child, we played kitchen, made tiny hotdogs and fries. Now she cooks meth, crushes Adderall, snorts coke, eats psilocybin mushrooms.

Later, she uses a knife to try and gouge out our brother's eyes.

When she is not running into the sea, cops find her running barefoot down highways. She is rushing against traffic as if to go back in time.

🔥

Manic again, my husband speaks a squall. Words turn faster than his tongue and he loses time. He is always going, gathering cloud and pressure, always moving further away.

From the windows I watch ice form on the lake only to crack, reminding me nothing is permanent.

My husband wanders onto the ice like danger is an illusion. His father and sister have disappeared when manic, hurtled as drivers down random roads or through the sky as passengers in great metal machines leading nowhere. Sometimes they said where they were going, but often not. Madness was why my husband's parents divorced when he was just a child. His sister went with his father; he was left behind with his mother's resentments.

This is partly why my husband does not want children. How can he rewrite a family narrative like that?

I am afraid my husband will leave me, run into the lake, down the highway, will drown us both in the rising waters of his madness. After more than a decade of these mercurial moods, sometimes I wish he would.

The red fox arcs like blood spatter through the snow. Its hunt for creatures beneath the snow is a reminder that things are living underground, buried and beating. Perhaps it is possible to resurrect the dead.

I fog the window with my wanting.

When the fox rises, a mouse dangles from the cage of its jaws. I imagine it alive, wonder if it is resisting or surrendering to the inevitable.

More than one student writes about self-harm. About the reassurance of pain. They write about their wounds. Like their missing classmate used to do.

My sister, too, seems to be lost; the line is dead.

After class, students scroll, heads down, as they stream into the hallways, stopping now and then like a clot. In the hour since class began, the news has announced that an iceberg has simply given up, slid from the solidity of land to swirl into oblivion. Deaths are mounting overseas from a new virus. The university emails to report a lecture series along with the latest student death from drinking, another sexual assault, this time a professor and a student, the punishment leave with pay.

At night when I walk back to my car in the dark, catcalls from the dorm windows sound like the coyotes that run through the woods around my house. I wake in the night to a pack screaming. Blood on the lawn.

Migraines from the low pressure of many storms feel like a premonition. The muscles around my neck tighten and coil. The space behind my eyes flashes. Agony pulses, reminds me that bodies exist to hurt.

It storms much of this fall and winter, leaving me roiling in the black and burst of migraines, which send me to a place that feels both real and otherworldly. It is impossible to escape the painful isolation of my skull.

I skirt the windows, desperate for the clouds to part. When the power goes out, like it does often on the East Coast, storms ravaging up the coastline like the tides, it goes so dark I see stars shatter behind my closed eyelids, hear my frantic heart. I am startled by the noise of being.

And by the intensity of the rain. The water fills up the wetlands that line the edge of my house, threatening to spill over.

&

When Hurricane Harvey hit, a woman I knew watched the water come for Texas, Louisiana. She drove between and beyond those borders with the ease of someone who took a cruise after the destruction because her insurance covered the damage.

She had faith enough to bring supplies to those in need. She posed, posted photos of the ways she tried to save those facing disaster. Mercy was always possible, her church preached, baptizing even the dead.

But animals were not people, she said, when she was asked to look after a pair of dogs. Their owner was out of town and the water was rising.

She left. They drowned, like much of the town.

&

In March 2020, we retreat indoors, tell ourselves we will wait out the virus that is here, everywhere. Time has slowed so we tread water.

We live by the sun's placement in the sky, by the red buds that form on the trees promising spring will return. We live inside like the woodland animals underground, fattening because eating is a comfort. There is no milk or flour. We are storing up for what is to come, hoping to wait out a winter whose end we cannot predict. Though they yank the groundhog from his hole and promise early spring, this warmth is just another sign of global heating.

Today the red cardinal looks like arterial spray in the snow. He rushes from branch to branch, crying out for a mate because spring is arriving and soon he will not matter. His tantrum against obsoletion might as well be our own, already whispers of a growing national resistance to quarantine, one that will allow us to continue to simply ignore impending extinctions, filthy rivers, corrosive rain, mountains collapsing on themselves because we gutted the insides.

I miss my student whose death feels a lifetime rather than a month ago. I miss the students I see now in their online posts, on my computer screen. Some have disappeared altogether, vanished as soon as the world changed. I wonder if they, like my absent sister, are alive.

Each morning I open my computer to dozens of close deaths among the hundreds, thousands, hundreds of thousands. Student emails sound like obituaries.

April is a rainy month, lightning piercing the sky to shards. A tree falls through a neighbor's roof and the walls simply cannot hold.

Onscreen a student sits in a flooding basement. Her family is upstairs, sick. She is waiting to see if she will be sick. She keeps her animals with her for comfort, but they balk at the flooding, panic, shriek.

🔥

Each night the water softener groans to life beneath our bed while my husband and I dream turned away from each other. He twitches in his sleep as if to run further, while my neck strains from looking back at the place from where we came, the smell of salt from the California sea.

It is hard, the water here, in the house we bought to save our marriage only to lock ourselves inside and watch the world fail.

The buried well hauls up minerals to the shower, plastered on like the scum around the sink drain, rusting orange no matter how we scrub it clean.

My husband dumps bag after bag of salt into the softener to grind the minerals down. The softener runs through the tank and pipes to smooth them like our bodies when we first met, licking loam and musk from beneath ears and throats. I miss our early years when we wrote our future together, when the world seemed to expand like our love. Now there is only silence, the story of our collective hurts, the world wounded too, shrinking until all that remains is wanting something that almost doesn't exist anymore.

Now we shower alone. Sometimes the softener goes off when I am in the shower and suddenly I am surrounded by both salt and my childhood fears of drowning in an unforgiving ocean because I was too stubborn to give myself up to the waves, fighting the current instead, believing nothing was stronger than my will.

The salt leaves a film over my skin, like I've been baptized, like the foggy way I move through the world after a month, then two months, and more, spent inside.

At night the tank empties salt water onto the back lawn outside our bedroom window. It pools and kills the grass. In the morning I watch birds peck at the brittle ground.

◊

I would swim across an ocean for my mother, but there is no water, only a continent between us. She claims one side of the country and I claim another.

Her daughter is still lost to addiction, two of her sons using, too, sneaking out of the house at night. Like our father—who refuses to wear a mask in a pandemic—they do not fear death.

My mother must close her business running a home daycare, but she does not know how she will survive without the money. Each day she watches the television scrolling disaster, and babysits her three-year-old granddaughter, my other sister too bored and beautiful to sit home and waste her twenties.

My mother paces her house, washes spiders and bugs from the potatoes because she cannot afford to buy a bag of fresh spuds, trapped with my restless father who is immune to her fear and the way she struggles to teach my siblings online.

On the opposite coast, I pace my empty, childless home, trapped with my restless husband who thinks my fears are unfounded. We both want a version of family the other does not, but still we try to want each other. The drug company stops making my birth control. I take Plan B and clutch at my stomach. Blood blooms in the toilet.

I see our neighbor, laid off from her job and home with her child who cries and pouts and cannot understand. Mornings while her husband works the wife sits in the cold, waiting for spring and the arrival of baby animals here—birds and bunnies, foxes and fawns. Afternoons, she tries to keep their child from crying while her husband mows the lawn, moves rocks about the yard, takes all of the tools out of his shed to wash and then put back. At night she cooks while he golfs. Eventually she stops coming outside.

I think of Noah's wife and his three daughters-in-law trapped on the ark, cleaning up after the animals, washing bugs from the potatoes because they cannot get any others, watching the restless men, the pacing lions that would crack their bodies beneath their fearful jaws if given that chance.

The women retreated into the hull of the ship to rock themselves and listen for the rustle of another heartbeat inside so that they might not feel so alone. Outside, the rain fell for forty days and forty nights, the water rising all around.

Amidst the plague, the animals return. In the early months of the pandemic, we retreat inside and they clamor out of the sea and woods. Fish swim up the Venice canals, now clear and smooth, crabs scuttling along the floor. Jackals sit in empty parks, lit up by the moon and the city skyline in Tel Aviv, Israel. Deer cross pedestrian crossings in Nira, Japan. In Istanbul, Turkey, goats and sheep walk along an airport highway two by two.

A sea lion pulls itself from the shore, makes its way to a Buenos Aires sidewalk. Deer, monkeys, wild boar. England, India, Corsica. Peacocks flash blue against the concrete skyline. Wild furred horses graze in front of indoor stadiums where people seek shelter. Buffalo roam empty streets. A cougar jumps an apartment building wall. Dolphins and sea cows swim up the bay.

People take photos from inside the safety of their homes. They press their faces to the glass. They witness the animals as if for the first time.

Some say the animals have come into the cities because they are looking for us, lonely for human companionship. Some say the animals have come into the cities because in our absence they finally feel safe. It's bound to be temporary, but everyone is talking about how carbon emissions have decreased. With decreased human movement, the earth has slightly decreased its cosmic vibration.

The animals are not looking for us—they are exploring an alternative timeline where no humans on the ark survived.

$$\diamond$$

Groundhogs surface from their self-imposed isolation to find the sun and the buds returned. They gorge on clover, eating away entire afternoons. They respond to winter simply by reducing the beat of their hearts.

Shuffling to the sweet spots, stuffing leaves in their cheeks, they freeze if a shadow moves overhead, scattering quickly when the neighbor's dog comes outside, barks, and struggles against her leash.

The neighbors adopt a dog because they are bored of being scared, or scared of being bored. The dog is afraid of men and people, wind and sticks. Her fear is my fear and I watch her through the fence while she tries to escape the rope they've tied around her neck. I want to release her to run into the woods after a smell or a hunger.

After a few weeks the dog is no longer new and they lock her in the enclosed patio where they can't hear her bark. She spends long days at the glass, crying at the world she cannot access, at her own reflection.

The neighbors are annoyed, embarrassed by her fear. They promise to spay her, give her Prozac. I say fear is what keeps us alive.

That's a lie.

I say nothing. I wince at the barking like the news or the shadow of a plane or hawk.

Then I swallow my antidepressants. I find the pill I fed my scared cat now spat out on the carpet, bright as a droplet of blood.

$$\diamond$$

Growing up, reading my children's Bible, the ark and the animals frightened me. The threat of extinction, the rising tide.

That the world would not forgive us our cruelty unless we repented was a lesson my adopted grandmother taught me. We needed to repent if we were to be saved.

Mercy, she said, was always possible.

When I was young, she read me the story of the water and we watched jellyfish billow off the California coast, pulsing like our hearts.

Now a machine beats her heart and she is tiny as a memory too painful to recall. She weighs no more than her bones: disappearance her reward for survival. Because of the virus, I have not seen her in a year and do not know when—or if—I will see her again.

In Massachusetts I am drowning, but the water never comes, just like back home in California. My adopted grandmother says the squirrels are gone, the birds too, and even her cat has died, though she fed him water with a dropper while he lay wasting in the skin of his body.

I do not tell her about the baby robin I found dead in my grass, the crawdad too far from home, parched and scuttling on my threshold. I do not say that I wanted a child. I do not admit my husband did not. I do not say that I blamed him, nursed resentment, when really, I agreed, decided the world is too cruel. I cannot say that I don't believe in mercy anymore.

It threatens to storm all spring but the rain never comes, only the migraines. The lawn remains brittle and dead, another dry storm threatening overhead.

I describe the beauty of my garden to my adopted grandmother, but all of these flowers are pretend. She says her Bible study group is not speaking to her because she believes the virus is real. The faithful deny the plague.

I promise their cruelty is only temporary; I promise the rain will return.

&

A new report sets an accelerated course for global heating. By then I will be as old as my mother is now, she as old as my adopted grandmother, all of us living out our final days convinced that the world is ending.

The Doomsday Clock moves to one hundred seconds to midnight.

One op-ed warns that having a biological child is the worst thing you can do to the environment. Another report says that mothers are suffering most during the pandemic. Still another describes the trauma of children raised in the crisis. A baby born in quarantine turns one and has spent so much time locked inside he cannot stand the stimuli of sun, of sound, is anxious and fretful in the outside world.

A neighborhood boy rides his bike outside my house every day to hide in my front bushes and cry. Another walks his dog with his head down, scrolling disaster (I assume) on his phone. He veers, unaware, from the path, wandering into the woods.

Next door, the couple ignores each other while the dog barks. The mother leaves for weeks and the father turns on the backyard sprinkler for his crying daughter, makes pretend rain.

🔥

A giant tortoise struggles in the tide. A yellow Maui songbird strangles silent. The river dolphin dies. So does a blue macaw, one that looks like the giants my mother-in-law keeps in her kitchen in a cage.

In 2019, the first mammal extinction is caused by global heating, with rising sea-levels flooding the habitat of the Bramble Cay melomys. Social media nicknames the last snail of its kind. Lonesome George goes viral before his end, which also finishes his species.

When the final white male rhino dies there will be no need to bring the last two females on board the ark. They will die before the storm gives out.

Is it lonelier to be the starving polar bear, the ice crumbling beneath its feet, or the videographer, already hurting from what hasn't happened, a haunting in reverse?

🔥

We are in the dark again because hurricanes ripple up the East Coast, taking out the trees that have stood for a hundred years in these woods.

In the Midwest, friends in Indiana and Nebraska are without power because a tornado has ripped through the states. A friend flies from California to Iowa because his aging father gets lost when he drives, wanders off in the night. They seek professional care, but they also know that those in assisted living are left even more vulnerable when storms knock out the electricity.

My mother calls and California is without power because it is on fire again. It is 116 degrees and she is inside without air-conditioning, curtains drawn to keep the ash out. This latest fire is near my sister's last known address, the one near the sea. No one has heard from her in months. Like everything else we love, she has simply disappeared.

I walk to the water to see the shore give way to the tide. All around are splintered branches. It looks like I am peering out from inside the hull of a boat or the fossilized remains of some great extinct beast's ribcage.

From her social distance, a neighbor complains the lake is too hot now to paddleboard with her tiny dog.

My phone pings. Already another storm is brewing in the ocean's belly.

۵

All summer I watch the groundhogs. I pretend their baby is my own, and nurse my wounds. I plant white flowers for the creature to feast upon, staring from the window at the way it falls asleep after eating, headfirst in the clover. I wonder if I should leave pans of water for it to drink, but I worry it will drown in my need.

One day, I look out the window and a red-tailed hawk is on the back lawn, hunkered down and intent. It roots around the grass at one of the entrances to the groundhog's tunnel. I flee the house by instinct, shouting and waving my arms, try to scare the hawk from its hunger, though I know that's not how wanting works.

I am hysterical, I know, intent on aiding this one survival if I can during a year of so much loss. I am desperate for the creature to endure into autumn when the world will die as winter returns, the creature hiding away, leaving me alone in the darkness. My husband, my mother, my adopted grandmother tell me I cannot stop nature, cannot control life or death. The skies darken; a storm is on the way.

I try to shoo the baby groundhog into safety, but it freezes in fear as though I am the threat. It must eat if it is to survive. Every afternoon is a chance to store for the approaching season. I cannot fix anything.

The hawk swoops just overhead. Behind the bird, the clouds begin to swirl, the wind rustling the many broken trees. I wish it would rain to end this standoff, but the summer has been unseasonably dry. Next door, the dog barks.

The baby groundhog will not retreat, nor the bird, so neither do I. I do not know whether to look down or up. Grabbing the garden hose, I make my own version of the rain on the brittle grass. The hog is alarmed as I try to frighten it into its burrow, only to soak the soft fur instead. I spray the swooping hawk. I spray into the unrelating sky, water building at my feet.

TUMBLE

ROSE QUARTZ

When Daddy says so, Mama goes silent. Her mouth makes a thin line, hard as rock, lips turning white under pressure.

I have to follow the rules too—no talk back, no tank tops, no bad words. Except this time. This time, Daddy says the directions are wrong, that Mama is wrong, that I'm old enough after all for a rock polisher, the kind that smooths away ugly, leaves gems beneath.

No making a mess doesn't matter this time, when Daddy and I dump rocks into the tumbler and the dust makes a cloud. No noise doesn't matter either because the rocks grate against one another, the machine lurching all night.

I dream of quartz clear as diamonds or the stars I spy from my bedroom window. I dream of machines, of breaking glass. When I wake, I can barely hear what they say about money or family or who is in charge. I can barely hear Mama's tears, Daddy's stern correction over the tumbler.

Weeks go by. Wearing a body down over time. I stare at the tumbler when I should be helping Mama while Daddy is away long hours at work. I imagine the rocks crashing down on top of each other, smoothing out the broken bits, making them shine.

Eventually Daddy opens the machine and pours a dozen tiny gems into my cupped hands. They are smooth as a secret, cool like quiet.

Rose quartz, Daddy points out, is a stone for me. But it is said the stone is for hearts, for mothers, for gentleness.

Pink and translucent. Hardened over time.

JASPER

The stone is a blood drop, rust and scream. It is the color of hurt, of help. It is opaque, like when I color with my crayon as hard as I can—my hand hurts but no paper shows through, no light when I hold it up to the sun.

I like the stone because it is the name of my grandmother's dog, an old terrier with wiry fur that makes loving him hard. Jasper has a dirty nose, crusted with dog food and scab. His tail is chewed to the quick, wet and raw, always in his mouth.

He is skittish, like I usually feel, so I follow him around my grandparents' dark house with the drawn curtains, trying to offer him comfort. He walks wide circles around my grandfather, who sits in his chair, stroke-silent and angry.

My grandmother is silent too, like her husband taught her during the alcoholic years before he lost his ability to drive to the liquor store. She is like flint—cloudy from too many years of sediment and stress, but with a smooth darkness beneath. One strike and she might spark.

Jasper is for healing, for strength, for courage. I palm red, weight in my hand.

TIGER'S EYE

Early mornings, I watch cartoons from Daddy's lap. My favorite is the tiger with a spring in his tail because he bounces higher than the trees, into the clear blue sky. He is not afraid, not tethered to anything, including the earth. He obeys no rules, even those of gravity. No one tells him what to do.

I like tigers because they do not need to clean and cook like Mama, whose work is never done. She carries my baby sister on her hip, stirring pots on the stove, answering phone calls, worrying over bills, while I adventure outside with Daddy. She vacuums the carpets, mops the floors, buys groceries while we look through my rocks. I like to pile them on top of each other until the weight proves too much and they come crashing down.

Tiger's eye is ringed with gold like my mother's finger. Daddy doesn't wear a ring because men don't wear rings just like they don't say sorry for shouting or throwing a plate of food or spending too much money without asking.

I show Daddy my tiger's eye, and we sing the song from my cartoon about having *Fun, fun, fun, fun, fun*. The striations in the rock are my favorite, the way they shift, turn on each other in the light. The rock was not pretty before it survived pressure, but now it is exactly what we want.

Tiger's eye has two relatives—hawk's eye and cat's eye—stones I am desperate to add to my collection, to pass to Daddy to admire. My rock collector book for children tells me they striate because they are full of asbestos fibers—danger runs in the silica family—the kind that make it so you can't catch your breath, so the whole world feels like it's springing onto your chest, and all of a sudden you're heaving and gasping like my Mama when she is overwhelmed and locks herself into the bathroom.

I place stones under the door for her—rough white quartz, silver chrome hematite like a time machine going to the future, my smooth golden tiger's eye, the one I like to hold tight in my fist when I can't sleep at night, the one I'll later learn is said to release fear and anxiety, to aid harmony and balance, help people make important decisions.

But she sounds like a stone thrown into the river, falling to the bottom, ripples moving outward.

AMETHYST

We crack the geode with a hammer to split it open. It reminds me of the book on my mother's shelf, the one about babies sliding from the wide legs of women, wonders that require pain.

On the outside the rock looks like nothing, but inside I can see pressure and time, crystal spines. I like way the crystal tips are rich in color, deep purple and jet, the inside of the cavern pulsing like a heart.

Where the crystals reach the surface is bleached and leached, and I wonder how much pressure it takes to transform something sad into sparkle.

Amethyst forms when lava gets too close to the surface, threatens to boil over. Geodes form around a cavern, lava surrounding a hole and transforming the empty. They are meant for clarity, for calm. They are meant to tranquilize. The purple color comes from iron, like the taste of blood when I bite my tongue or Daddy cuts into a steak.

I have to be careful, Daddy says. Exposing the geode to light will fade the color. It is only pretty because it was buried so deep.

I like the musty smell of the geode, the way it smells like a memory. I run my hands across the crystals to feel the potential for hurt.

RED PUMICE

My grandmother's lonely house is lined with prickly bushes that dare you to touch them. All around, red pumice to hold the roots from running away. Though my grandmother has a lush garden in the backyard, one that trails past the fence bordering the property as if she is preparing to leave, nothing much grows in the front.

The pumice is light as the breath my grandmother sucks back into her throat when she forgets and speaks up, when my grandfather glares at her from his chair and she swallows her sorry to form a pit in her stomach.

The pumice is full of holes, tiny tracks to nowhere that I stare into, finding only dark and dust. When my mother brings me along to visit her parents, returns to crouch in the shadows of her childhood, suddenly skittish like her mother and the dog, I go outside and use my nails to pluck bits of prickly bush, sucking at the blood under the half-moons. I stuff the green into the holes so that the rock becomes a mountain, strong and tall and verdant. I cup the new world I've made in my palm.

No one cares about pumice. It doesn't have a meaning, doesn't stand for anything. A rock, like so many things, must be pretty to bear significance.

I've memorized the book pages that say pumice is created when volcanos eject super-heated, highly pressurized rock from their guts. The rocks cool quickly, shocked by the force of their expulsion, the rapid decrease in heat and pressure when they escape. Depressurization creates bubbles that freeze, minerals hardening around those hollows.

I love pumice because it survived, transformed. But I know it is worthless, only used for filing feet, cleaning toilets.

When I go inside, I know better than to bring my creations because my grandfather will be moody, my mother will be silently hunched over the hollow of her hurt. My grandmother fearful and resolute, her cigarettes billowing smoke and ash in the air, the lava glow threatening to burn her mouth.

Later I ask Daddy if we can put pumice into the rock polisher, if there is a way to make something that has survived so much into something pretty.

No, Daddy says. It would crumble to dust, disintegrate to nothing.

Black River Rock

Daddy's stone shines silver as a coin. It's his lucky rock, Daddy says, making his own meaning of the talisman, placing it in his pocket each morning with his wallet, his knife, his many keys. It keeps him safe on construction sites where men put nails through their fingers and break toes in steel-lined boots.

The rock is as big as my palm, bigger than most of my collection, heavy and cumbersome, but Daddy says it is special and I see how it shines, rubbed silver by his keys in his pocket all those years. It is warm from Daddy's heat, smells like metal and sawdust. Daddy holds it like the worry stones he gave me because I'm not sure about math and strangers, scared of the dark and people staring, bugs and sleepovers.

I don't know what Daddy worries about because Mama does the worrying while Daddy works, and when she tries to talk about fears he says shush and she does like her mom and all the women I know, their worry a hard edge, like the lines in their faces, that must be polished away.

Obsidian

"Careful," Daddy says. "I know you love it, but it can hurt you."

I hold the rock tight because it is my only one, but I feel the rough edges. It hurts to grip so hard, but I'm afraid I will lose it if I let go.

Obsidian is jet black and slick, like an oil spill or a mistake. Reflective and smooth, it reminds me of the glass bottles my parents' liquor comes in—nearly opaque, light fighting to get through.

At night they drink and Mama gets happy and Daddy doesn't mind if she shares her opinions on the bills or his brothers or politics because drink-talking is just pretend, liquid swishing around in a bottle so dark it might as well not be there at all.

When the family gets together, the men drink in the living room and tell bad jokes I'm not supposed to hear and not allowed to say, and the women drink in the kitchen, stirring food on the stove and sighing "I wish he wouldn't say that" in between swigs.

My grandfather falls asleep with his mouth open like a geode, his dentures bright stalactites and stalagmites in that cavern. I'm afraid to wake him when the women send me to his side, afraid he'll grumble like he does at my mother, who shakes him gently, gently, asking "Daddy?" at his stone face that so closely resembles her own.

I'm afraid he'll grip my arm like he does my grandmother's, his fingerprints on her skin long after he lets go. To ease him from sleep I offer my stone collection, hand him aventurine, milky and green as jade, and my smallest piece of turquoise. He asks for my rainbow hematite, galactic and metal, and I hand it over because I am not allowed to say no.

Sometimes I put a stone at each place on the table, the prettiest opal for Mama, Daddy's favorite pyrite, obsidian for myself. Obsidian is for truth-telling, for protection. It comes when magma explodes wide open, goes slick and spiked in the sky.

Sometimes I gather ugly stones from the yard and color them in with markers, a special color for each member of the family. I put glitter nail polish over the top to make them shine like they are real. At the beginning, everyone says "How pretty" but when they drink more and more, no one notices, and later Daddy says I've made a mess.

Mornings, I take trash bags of bottles out to the recycling. Sometimes I open them and peer through the end of the bottles like I do through my obsidian, watching the light struggle and refract.

CRAZY LACE AGATE

Agate looks like my tummy feels, all twists and turns with no end, no clear path out.

It looks like Mama talking to Daddy when he won't understand, no matter how slow she talks, how sweet she makes the words sound, silver and milk-smooth like marble. It looks like his face scrunching up to interrupt, correct, say "not now" or "no" or "I'm busy."

It looks like my father's brothers, drunk on the couch, the smell of beer and cigarette smoke and sweat sharp throughout the house. It looks like how I love them so much it hurts because it's like having three rough and tumble Daddies but I can't seem to ever wake them, or how my aunts spend all morning in the bathroom with hairspray and perfume getting pretty for eyes that are already glazed and crazed.

Agates protect against negativity, promote confidence, unlock tongues to tell the truth. They are used for the courage to start over.

Agates come in all colors—tans and blue, green and red—but mine is cream and lavender, like a bruise. Like the waitress's eyeshadow when my father's father grabs her behind as she leans forward with my pancakes.

My pancakes are flat as an agate slice and I pour thick syrup over the top until they shine like polished rock. It tastes good, but after too long the syrup crusts on the plate, goes hard and brown like tar. I drag my fork through like an animal caught in the pits. Rocks aren't the only thing that transform with lava, with heat and pressure. I've seen the bones of animals trapped—frozen in fear, unable to run.

Animals run from my father's brothers like the dog runs from my mother's father, like my pets run from my father. They make crazy agate paths in the rug until the men shout and stomp, sometimes kicking them in the soft sides, the smell of smoke and perfume all around. When the women say "stop" the men say "quiet."

Crazy connects all the sides of the family with those who married into it. Once, on my mother's side of the family, my step-cousin put car oil in the dog water bowl, wild spirals slick at the surface. The oil came from dead animals in the ground, my rock book said. The dog died. A few weeks later, his father, my uncle, used the car with the new oil to run over his ex-wife.

She talked too much, shouted during an argument, didn't listen when he said "shush," so he ran his car up and over her body, crushed her bones, and when my tummy feels twisty and sick, like if I stare too close at my agate, everyone says its ok because he told the judge he didn't do it but if he did it was because she deserved it.

Before my uncle goes to jail and my mother's sister moves far away to start over somewhere safe, I give him one of my most special rocks. But later, when I hide under the crazy blanket Mama crochets from yarn scraps, my worry stone beneath my pillow, all I see is the twists and turns of his car down the long, dusty drive.

BLUE AGATE

My blue geode present comes split, a clean line severed between one side and the other.

The crystals are small and delicate as sugar, the color bright, likely dyed. Any fluorescent agate is typically manufactured by boiling the stone, leaving it in a strong solution that will penetrate any cracks and take over. The stone, weakened over time, simply accepts the color, transforming by demand.

The center cavern is as small as my finger, as small as I feel sometimes, afraid to say what I think or feel because I see what happens when girls and women let secrets out of the caves of their mouths.

The geode is a trick. Put the pieces together and it looks whole, hides the hollow inside.

BLACK GRAVEL

Eventually I will grow, move away, leave my mother in the house with my father, his brothers and mine, the many men in our extended family cold as stone but sparking like flint when my mother speaks, dares to disagree. As a child, I used pumice to rub her feet smooth, the dead bits falling like ash to the ground. But after I leave, she will stop trying to walk tender, growing hard and cracked instead.

When the California drought gets years-long, Daddy will replace our grass with gravel. I will visit and be unable to recognize my home, surrounded by stone. The gravel will be dull in the sunlight, my childhood gemstones long disappeared.

At night I will struggle to sleep with the sound of the dryer, clothes tumbling over themselves until the last of the water is gone. I will think of my childhood, standing at the polisher with my father, delighted by the sound of disintegration, a body broken over time.

I will imagine my mother watching silent. The way she worried I might get hurt, that I was not old enough for this machine, that I might grow to believe everything capable of being shined to sparkle.

As an adult I will stand with my mother and the women in the kitchen, my father and the men in the living room. When the women speak politics, ideas, hurt, my father will shout from the other room, says "quiet" or "shush" or "no thank you" in a singsong that does not mean fun. When I speak, he will wave his hands in my face, interrupt, say "no" as though I am a child except I will be a woman. I will go silent as granite, feeling cracked in two.

Outside, gravel will cover as far as I can see—bland filler for when a landscaper doesn't have the patience to nurture growth. Rocks used to crush out weeds, to suffocate what tries to flower.

PYRITE

Daddy's favorite rock does not come from the polisher. He delivers it to me from inside his heavy hand and it shines among the lines of his palm. Golden, precious.

Pyrite brings luck and prosperity. It shields the user from criticism.

Daddy shares his rock with me so I will be good. So I will help Mama with the cooking and the cleaning and the crying. When I lick the rock with the smooth tip of my tongue, I believe I taste abundance.

I do not realize pyrite is the most abundant sulfide mineral, that it is a major contaminator of groundwater, that when oxidized, pyrite releases poisons like arsenic. I do not know it is gold for a fool.

I store this stone for Daddy among my treasures, fetch it for him when he asks, hide it under his pillow, in his work boots that take him away so often.

I keep my voice silent which means good which means stay which means please love me.

I hold my body still. I turn to stone hoping I will shine.

TAKING STOCK

Shortly after I was born, my older brother pulled out the gun he had been gifted by a relative, aimed at his stomach, and pulled the trigger.

The bullet ricocheted through his wiry sixteen-year-old frame.

My parents heard the shot from the kitchen where they were making dinner and watching me in my infant chair. But they didn't recognize the sound or register what happened until my brother came out from his room clutching his wound, leaving a trail of blood. The ambulance came, wailed him away to the hospital.

He lived.

As a child I did not understand the thick keloid that crawled across my brother's stomach like a terrible creature. Raised and smooth except where it puckered to attach, my brother's scar was a secret. He called it his worm whenever I asked, which was often, because he did not come home to visit as much as I wished, ignored me when he did though I clung to him, desperate for his indifferent love. He would never tell me where the scar came from, what it meant, insisted it was a worm crawling across his abdomen like a pest, something that would one day wander away.

Years later I discovered the truth. He did not want a half-sister, and when he discovered his girlfriend was pregnant and overheard my father talking to the young girl's father on the phone, he preferred death to becoming a parent so young. He was afraid of becoming like our father, who turned eighteen the day after my brother was born.

I do not mind that my brother recoils at the sight of me. Now I can understand that I am a reminder of that violence, a symbol of the way he switched off the safety and tried to die.

But what has bothered me these many long years after my brother survived and my parents got rid of that gun is why my father kept a gun of his own tucked away as if the damage had not been done.

◊

Gunshots ring out in my backyard.

It is early Saturday morning, the sun barely visible above the lake, the world soft and velvet, mist clinging to the Massachusetts woods. Out every window, wilderness: birch, maple, pine.

My husband and I bought this home in the forest to escape. To flee the noise and news—everywhere, it seemed, danger. Here we live small in a place where trees stretch large into the sky. Our home rests on a few solitary acres, surrounded by woods and wetlands. Down a private road, it is not visible to those who don't know it exists. Days pass where we see no humans except each other.

Instead, wild turkeys and great blue herons, does and their wobbly fawns, foxes and coyotes playing on the lawn, groundhogs and chipmunks, bounding rabbits and squirrels, fierce fisher cats and red-tailed hawks. The forest is full of life, wild asparagus and raspberries bursting up each spring, a dozen kinds of bees and dragonflies filling the air with their vibrant color and sound, bats and owls swooping low in the dusk. Though I grew up in rural California, I never understood the thrumming wild until moving to the woods.

We chose this place, too, because it is surrounded by conservation land, protected forests that will not be harvested to make way for pavement or another cul-de-sac.

But Massachusetts permits hunting on its protected lands and so each morning during the hunting season, I wake to gunfire. It echoes through the stillness, rattling my windows. My body tenses instinctively, the hairs on my arms raising like my cats' backs, poised for danger.

I think of the fawns I've watched all spring, the ones barely old enough to venture into the meadow on their own now, their soft muzzles coated in clover. Or the wild turkey that set up roost in the mid-

130

dle of our yard this spring, sauntering through the brush and coming close to the window to look at us and the cats, to show off his glorious call and feathers. The fox who pounces the yard for mice or fun when it snows and he leaps headfirst, a bright streak lighting up the lonely.

Nothing seems safe.

Our property stretches several acres into the woods and wetlands. There is no boundary where the conservation land ends and our land begins. I worry the hunters will not know, would not care, will stalk the ducks they hunt each fall as close as they need to the house to ensure a kill.

In the New England autumn, the trees seem to bleed, and the sound of gunshots ricochet in the chambers of my heart.

🔥

Above our sleeping child bodies, the walls are lined with the heads of the dead. Bucks with glassy eyes, turkeys stuffed and sprayed to glisten. Someone's father has a taxidermied skunk, another has a glossy duck with an emerald green head.

Fathers in our rural California town leave each fall, driving their dusty pickups to Kansas or Montana where there is easier access to hunting and game, death a sport. They return with stories and the promise of a good mount, jerky to pull with our strong teeth, a freezer full of flesh to last the mild winter.

Our middle school sleepovers take place under a five-point buck, his stoic gaze protecting us from the ghost stories we share long into the night. We talk about the boys at school, the ones who go paintballing every day, stalking one another like prey through the sunny fields, blasting bright splotches of red and blue across each other's limbs, raised welts and bruises bleeding across their arms. They wear camouflage like our fathers, heavy boots, artillery vests.

Though they play with paint, eventually they will inherit their father's guns, will build their arsenals—AK-47, AR-15—and hang machine gun rounds from the posters of their beds. They will upgrade to bulletproof vests, will treasure old grenades, relics. They will modify fireworks and build bombs on the weekends and slur, "I could kill

131

anything," when they slide next to us on the couch, smelling sharp like beer, gripping their hands around our thighs.

A dozen deer heads line the walls of my best friend's living room, antlers casting shadows when we turn out the lights. Her father hangs heads in the dining room too, and his office, where he forgets his work at the nuclear power plant, the threat of danger, the way he moves throughout the day on edge. Hunting is his catharsis, measured stalking, steady aim, mediation in massacre. His office walls display dozens of guns, long bows, bullets, bodies. He keeps the door closed, like his ears when we try to talk to him, or his face when his wife speaks, but when he forgets and leaves the door open, we glimpse his trophies lining those dark walls.

At school we are encouraged to compete for trophies too, every student required to participate in the Future Farmers of America. My best friend raises sheep, great wooly clouds that run to the fence when she arrives with the feed, prancing around the pen after her like a shadow.

When the time comes to butcher, my friend cries and cries, mourns the loss of her pets to a gunshot. But the pay is good, so the next year and the next, she raises lambs for slaughter.

I do not understand when my professor freezes. He is a renowned author, a prominent speaker, but a new student on the first day of class makes him afraid.

The student is not in our MFA program, instead auditing the course because he has a novel to write about his time in Afghanistan, a war story with bombs and guns and a hundred deaths and a weary soldier.

He shares this, interrupting, growing aggressive when the professor tries to return us back to the syllabus. The student cracks his knuckles, shifts restless in his seat. At the break, he rushes the professor in the hall.

The next class, the soldier is gone and the professor walks us to a new room, a new building, which we are to keep secret. At the time, I think him paranoid.

I have just started teaching, barely twenty-one and mimicking professor at the front of the class. My students bring me mixed CDs and visit my office hours to talk about bands the they like—Panic! At the Disco, Death Cab, The Killers.

I am young and afraid of failure, but never of my students.

Because I am so young, so distracted and convinced of my own importance, I do not realize that my professor worked at Virginia Tech before coming to my school in California's Central Valley. I barely registered the Virginia Tech massacre when it occurred the previous spring because it was so far away from my small California college near the beach where nothing dangerous ever happened except drunk boys who wouldn't listen to no. An English major killed 32 people and wounded 17 others with two semi-automatic pistols before shooting himself in the head, but I do not realize my professor knew those barricaded in classrooms, students jumping from windows trying to escape and professors who, after the incident, reported the student-turned gunman as having been "odd," said they should have known. They knew.

When the massacre took place, I was graduating from college, preparing for graduate school in the fall, shocked anyone thought me suited to stand in front of a class. I drove the long hours to my new grad school to visit my old friend at her nearby university apartment. We drank wine and talked about how I would be joining her there soon and how her father still went on long hunting trips alone, how she didn't have much to say to him anymore, how she was a vegetarian now after killing so many sheep.

We didn't talk about the Tech massacre. We didn't think anything bad could happen to us, though we also didn't talk about the men we knew who grew angry, violent, wrapped their hands around our necks, raised welts and bruises bleeding across our arms.

Less than a month after the Virginia Tech shooting, this same friend called crying. There had been a shooting in her apartment building. A student was dead and two others injured over a PlayStation game.

Police stretched yellow caution tape across the death scene, an apartment a few doors down the hall from my friend's. She did not need to describe where it was—I remembered. I was visiting the day before, had walked past the open door, the sound of their game, their mock gunfire, echoing down the hall after me. I waved at the boys inside as though we were friends.

◊

At home, the boys love me because I let them shoot me.

I have lots of practice babysitting elementary school boys who shoot me with Nerf Guns, the bright foam bullets grazing my arms, bouncing off my back. The kids shoot me when I'm cooking, when I'm cleaning, when I help them with their homework. They shoot me when they should be sleeping. They shoot me when my back is turned, but their favorite time to shoot me is when I am right in front of them and hold up my arms for protection, say, "Too close. No." They like to fire most when I say, "Please don't shoot."

When my new brothers move in from foster care, my parents must sign a form that says they understand my brothers have witnessed trauma. That the boys have been abused by angry parents and strangers, bones and brains broken and rebuilt around the scars. My brothers are young, two and three, but already they are angry, slapping our faces after they hold out their arms to hug us, pinching themselves so hard they bleed, punching themselves in the face and laughing, wrapping their hands around their necks until they are breathless. They kick the family dog, try to hang the family cat. They try to hurt us and pretend it was an accident. They step on every bug, kill all their toys. When we ask why, they stare and say matter-of-factly, "God wants them to die."

We know something is wrong from the start. When they finally begin to speak, some of their first words are "kill" and "dead."

In elementary school they collect bullet casings and sharp rocks. They start fires in the house and break the bones of their classmates.

In high school they take knives to school and shatter their classmates' bodies on concrete, blood spattering on their shoes. They say they will get revenge; they speak of bombs.

When they are suspended or bored, they put their fists or their heads through walls.

They charge at the cops who come to arrest them, fight their probation officers and psychiatrists. They are locked up—and released—again and again.

They will stab us, shoot us, they say, their eyes wild and dead all at once. They pull weapons out of the holes they've made in their mattresses; they pick the lock to the closet where my father secures his gun.

My parents try everything to help—therapy, medication, new schools, family counseling. My brothers push my mother, lunge to watch her recoil. My brothers threaten my father. Because they are wards of the state and on probation for drugs and weapons, my parents cannot remove them from the home. The paper trail of their threats, their violent outbursts, the psychiatrists and probation officers who say they are "too disturbed" to keep working with these boys stretches back many years.

I wonder what we will look like if—when—my brothers commit the violence they have craved for as long as I've known them. Will we stand in the doorway and give a statement to reporters? Will we say we should have—that is, have always—known?

I ask the dentist to turn off the TV positioned in front of my face, the one designed to distract from the numbing, from the scrape of a blade and the pain of a drill.

But the office—like the country—is captivated.

We watch from the safety of a dental office in Massachusetts, watch the dazed faces of students and teachers in Parkland, Florida, the panic behind their eyes, the way they try not to cry so they will seem composed in this chaos. Reporters are already assembling the facts: 17 dead, 17 injured, semi-automatic rifle, an adopted high school dropout enrolled in Junior ROTC with a long history of violence to himself and others, a history of killing animals, open threats to kill people with guns.

His classmates and teachers say authorities should have known. From 2008 to 2017, police received at least 45 calls about the shooter. On February 5, 2016, an anonymous tip reported that he threatened to shoot up the school. On November 30, 2017, another call said he might be a "school shooter in the making" and that he collected knives and guns. On September 23, 2016, a peer counselor notified the school resource officer of his suicide attempt and intent to buy a gun.

In 2019, the story is all too familiar. Over the course of 46 weeks of this year, there have been 45 school shootings. We want the story to stop, so in the weeks that follow we hope that the students at Marjory Douglas Stoneman High School—the ones who plead for change on television each night, the ones who organize the March for Our Lives while lawmakers are still sending thoughts and prayers or running from reporters to avoid commenting at all—will assume the responsibility adults abandoned long ago.

All too soon, however, it will become clear that nothing will be done, and the tragedy will simply sink to the bottom of the news cycle.

But for a moment, on that February afternoon in the dentist's office, everyone—dentist, hygienists, receptionists—stands still to watch. The appointment, the world, pauses. My body, my mouth, forced to comply. Even as I try to avert my eyes, I am pinned to the chair, mouth open in a silent scream.

The first time I shoot a gun is for a school project.

"You've written a lot about your aversion to violence," my undergraduate professor says. "Why not study responsible gun ownership to challenge your beliefs?"

This project will not change my beliefs, but I am dutiful to my GPA. I tell my boring boyfriend and he tells his boring friends, the ones who shoot guns in video games, cackling over their headsets and the virtual carnage.

Our friend has a rifle and a few handguns. We go to his house in the rolling hills of California and stand overlooking the pool and the vineyards. The guns are lined up next to the sunscreen on a lounge chair.

I am apprehensive but everyone says it's as easy as a videogame. "Haven't you played *Call of Duty*?" they ask. "It's like *Grand Theft Auto*."

I know that game, the one designed around stealing cars, where gamers can shoot anyone—civilians, police, prostitutes.

"What's the point?" I ask my boyfriend. "What are the consequences?"

But I should already know. The police only come after you, my boyfriend explains, if you are a bad guy.

"Sure, if you shoot, the police come," he explains, never taking his eyes from the screen, the sound of gunfire and screaming. "But if you're good at the game, the police eventually give up."

My friend's doctor father comes outside to supervise.

I shoot the rifle first, hold it firm against my shoulder. I know I shouldn't, but I close my eyes in order to summon the courage to pull the trigger. The sound cracks through my protective ear coverings, the kickback causing me to nearly drop the gun. I am shaky with what I have done, the way I've pierced the sky.

All around, the boys cheer.

It is easier to shoot the pistol. It fits in my hand, could even fit in my tiny purse next to my bobby pins and lip gloss. Because I want this to be over, I shoot without hesitation. My hands vibrate with the power.

When I am done, I feel the same, but I dutifully write a paper about all that I've learned.

By the end of the day, I can barely lift my arms, purple bruise swelling across my shoulder.

🔥

Like her name, she is Honey sweet, sidling up to my desk before and after class to ask about the assignment, to tell me about her military boyfriend, her horses, her spot on the rifle team. The first in her family to go to college, like me, she is desperate to succeed, to belong.

She stands out from her classmates with her bulky clothes and braces, her rural upbringing. She struggles to make small talk with anyone. I pair her up with the friendliest students, including another student on the rifle team, one so tiny she can barely hoist the gun, so anxious she has panic attacks in class and cries in my office, desperate for an anxiety medication but is prohibited to take calming prescriptions during competitive shooting season.

But Honey will not talk to her. She will not talk to anyone besides me, both of us poor rural kids out of place at this big university, desperate to belong yet unsure how to camouflage ourselves enough to fit in. Behind her eyes is a silent sad.

Here in Nebraska, where I teach at the large state university around which all things—like sports and politics—seem to revolve, it is the fall of 2016. The students are first-time voters, a mixture of rural farm kids and midwestern city students well-versed in contemporary politics. Despite what most assume about Nebraska, the class is diverse—Black students, Latinx students, queer students, disabled students, international students from Sudan and South Korea, nontraditional students with college-age children of their own. That Honey appears quintessentially Nebraskan is what isolates her.

As the presidential election approaches, the students are on edge, talking before and after class about their fears. Honey, silent all semester, suddenly speaks. She tells her classmates they are wrong. She raises her voice over her classmates of color, over queer students, over me when I intervene.

Soon she begins discussing her guns, her impeccable aim, the way she slaughtered animals over the weekend with ease. She raises her voice so we all can hear. A few times she brings her rifle to class, for though guns are banned on campus, exceptions are made for competitors. She wears a red trucker hat, dangling rifle earrings, jewelry made of bullets.

Her classmates do not want to work with her and their hesitation makes her bold. She approaches their desks, will not leave when they will not respond or look her in the eye. She stays after class to ask me about politics and when I will not tell her who I am voting for or talk about the presidential debates because they are not on our syllabus she says, "I'm a consumer."

She will not be ignored—not by me, not by her rifle teammate, not by the students who sit together and laugh at her conspiracy theories. Then, one day, in the middle of a class discussion, she bursts into angry tears, spits out, "Just wait. You'll see."

After class, I talk in the hall with other teachers, all of us graduate students who are often told we dramatize classroom tensions, who are lectured that we need to work on our authority in the classroom. We decide I should say nothing. A few years later, one of the friends who says, "It's probably fine" will be locked in a classroom, hiding behind a desk with her students while an active shooter rains gunfire across the campus.

On election day Honey arrives in full camouflage, her hair pulled back like she is hunting. She sits on the edge of her seat like she is spotting her target. She laughs to no one.

When she is right and we are wrong, when she wins and we lose, she goes silent again, smug and satisfied. A bullet dangles at her throat.

◊

They keep the funeral casket closed after my friend shoots himself in the head with a rifle.

It is the first death in our high school, the first suicide, just like my friend is—was—the first openly gay kid in our rural town.

At the funeral, his parents and the preacher take turns addressing the high school, which has canceled for the morning so we can all attend. They take turns telling us they can't decide which is worse—that he was gay or that he shot himself.

◊

The first year I arrive in Massachusetts, a student writes about shooting into the dead body of a lynched man.

His essays tell the story of his military service in New Orleans post-Katrina, how the soldiers found the bloated bodies of the dead, hung black men from trees at the entrance to their base, a bullet required for entry.

He was disgusted, he says. He did it anyway, he admits.

He dreams of guns, of death, including his own. His essays work through the violence of military service and toxic masculinity, grappling with a country that glorifies guns as a sign of patriotism and freedom. He is a brilliant student, a kind man.

It is hard to imagine him in the landscape he describes—the

murky rising waters, the floating garbage and faces, the way the bodies were heavy enough he had to hoist them on top of him in the boat, resting beneath the weight.

The following year I don't recognize him when he sits in my classroom. He is pale and numb like the New England fall, dark and quick to storm.

He laughs one minute, snaps at his classmates and me in the next. He picks strange fights over fonts and music opinions. The many women in class will not sit by him. I realize I've become afraid each time I open the door.

As per university policy, I make one report, then two. I schedule meetings to talk to my superiors, who tell me it is very concerning.

One day the soldier stands up when he shouts, the camouflage he has been wearing to class lately doing nothing to conceal his rage. He sputters, interrupts, loses his train of thought, cries angry tears while he points around the room, red-faced, pacing like a wild animal.

After the incident, which I report yet again, I am required to meet with him. He comes to my office and cries and says, "Please help me, no one understands."

He has been reported, he says, by disability services because they think he is violent, a threat, because the employees there are afraid to work with him. He says he thinks they are probably afraid he has a gun. He says that because he is a solider everyone is afraid he has a gun. He cries and says he does not want people to be afraid of him, gripping the edge of my desk so I can see the bones through the flesh, the sinew pulling.

He says he is banned from entering the building. He says he hasn't slept in days but actually it is months. He says he is so angry and scared and trapped now that they have done this to him and now he will be marked forever as a threat. He says this will go on his record like all the other times the university thought he was dangerous.

I am also his academic advisor and he wants me to see if the report is on his record. There is nothing. Just like there is nothing from the reports I've made. I tell my department chair and we will file another report when this is over, when he is done hanging his head in his hands and crying and saying *help me* and then *fuck you* and then *I want to disappear*.

He does disappear, even though he is only a semester away from graduation. And because the enrollment numbers are low, we are expected to reach out to him, tell him we want the best for him, that we hope he returns.

I do not want him to return, nor do his classmates who email me to say they are afraid. One student comes to my office, says she has an adopted brother who is violent, in and out of police custody. "He reminds me of being afraid," she says of the soldier, hanging her head. And I know because he reminds me of my brothers too.

More than a decade after I start teaching, I walk my Massachusetts students to a new room, a new building, which I ask them to keep secret. As we walk across campus in the rain, I hope they don't think I am paranoid.

◊

My backyard gives way to woods, and a public hiking trail if you walk far enough through the dark bramble.

The trail meanders along the edge of the lake until it splits, stretches deep into a forest so dense that in summer you can look up at the sky and see nothing but green, and in winter you can look up at barren branches that make it seem as though you are held by the bones of the dead.

I walk here when I want to disappear. When the world seems too much and too cruel. When the sound of gunshots on the news, movies, videogames, music becomes so loud I can barely breathe.

Today I head toward the trail because the news reports that another man has been shot by police, after the man yesterday and the woman last week. This week there has been another school shooting and one in the mall. Last week an active shooter roamed my California hometown for several days, my parents calling me because they could not believe it was happening in our rural area. Because they saw my brothers when they looked into the dead-eyed photo posted on the news.

I leave my woods and approach the trail, sunlight piercing now and then through the trees. It is spring, the branches blooming with life, pollen raining through the air, butterflies and bees vibrating, the sound of robins overhead and ducks lazing in shallow pools of water. I breathe a sigh of relief and turn the corner.

Standing at the entrance to the trail is a man dressed in camouflage, his hunting rifle pointed straight at my face.

IN PRAISE OF THE PLAINS

In summer, Nebraska skies splinter, lightning wrecking the blue dome, shattering it to shards. Storms come on sudden, though the birds know and take to the skies in a cackle, wings beating warning. At first, storms seep in yellow at the horizon's edge before blackening the afternoon, barometrics pressing down, and then a funnel forms, twisting like a child's cartoon tangle angling towards town. Sirens wail, hail dents car hoods, a tree goes through the ceiling, nature overtaking the living room, dripping wet and verdant. And visible through the branches and open ceiling: a fearsome sky wracked with fire.

When I moved to the Great Plains from California's central coast, where the shoreline dips like the dimple of a lover's flesh, the estuary foggy and safe, the weather moderate, I was fascinated and terrified. On the coast, summers were temperate, peaking in the 80s, night lows sinking to the 60s, beach picnickers' deepening tans the only indicator the earth was turning, that the sandy moment was not the center of the universe. Kelp washed in with the waves, great undersea forests easily uprooted to line the beach with their briny smell, and ice plants dotted the sand with their succulent flesh and bright flowers, though why they were named for a cold that never came, we did not know. Winters, too, were mild, reaching lows of 40, highs in the 60s or 70s, picnickers still lining the beaches, wrapped in blankets as they fed gulls bits of bread, surfers still paddling out on the waves rushing in.

But the Plains—which encompass the entirety of the U.S. states of Kansas, Nebraska, North Dakota and South Dakota, as well as parts of

Colorado, Iowa, Minnesota, Missouri, Montana, New Mexico, Oklahoma, Texas and Wyoming—were contradictory and cruel. Accustomed to the marine layer fog of the coast, which made the landscape appear like an Impressionist painting, some Monet or Cassat, all soft light and diffuse color, I assumed weather to be generally benevolent. But winters in Nebraska were cold and dark, and venturing outside reminded me of my small, animal body whose advanced opposable thumbs were simply no match for nature that reached -30 degrees, turning red then blue in a mere matter of moments, as if they might snap.

When the snow came—my first—I assumed all snowfall would follow a similar pattern, moving along a scale from tolerable to worse until the most awful storm of all, which would bring the reward of a snow day and allow me to stay indoors in front of a fire, looking out the window at a landscape like Brueghel's quaint scenes of snowy villages. But the weather was not so simple and snowfall, I found, came in more ways than I could have imagined. There was soft snow that fell as I was walking about in town, glistening on my coat or hair for a moment, looking lovely until it left me damp—a small price to pay for the glittering moment. There was snow that came in large clumps, dotting my living and soaking me through in an instant. There was snow that fell fast and iced the road, left me sliding across sidewalks like a figure skater without sequins. There was snow that fell lightly as though dancing down to join us; snow that fell in flurries, whipping and spinning in time to some unheard music; snow that fell at blunt angles, hard and harsh; snowstorms that blocked out what little sun the winter months permitted, sweeping over the land like a heavy blanket, making it hard to move and breathe, leaving the world clouded and surreal, lines of wet white rushing by at all angles, a Jackson Pollock, multilayered, intense, chaotic.

Weather on the Plains was a force on its own, controlling the people and determining how we would spend our days, how, in essence, we would live. If Nebraska was one of Brueghel's landscapes, surely it was *The Fall of Icarus*, our hubris dashed by the indifference of nature. There was no control here; this place was not easy to love.

The Plains are a place of extremes—tornados and blizzards, heat waves and deep freezes, thunder without rain. Weather on the

Plains is mercurial—unstable, unpredictable, and fascinating in this. The Plains have some of the hottest summers and coldest winters, some of the largest temperature swings anywhere, some of the fiercest droughts and blizzards, the shortest growing season, plus fierce hail storms and fires, even plagues of locusts. The Plains resist empathy or understanding, demanding instead that we stand in awe. Storms rip towns open at the vein with little mercy, the history of early settlers— Belle Starr, Butch Cassidy and the Sundance Kid, the Bloody Benders of Kansas, Calamity Jane, Jesse James, the violence committed against Indigenous populations—showing that to live, grow, and thrive here is not easy.

Each season I waited for what the weather would do. Spring came and went in a matter of weeks, along with my coastal assumption that spring, like summer, was a mass of picnics and ocean kayaks, barbeques and bike rides, beach days and bonfire nights. One moment the Plains were frozen, great heaps of snow steeped at the side of the road, slick black from exhaust, and the next they were molten, the humidity a wet heat I'd never known, suffocating and exhausting. No one, it seemed, went out much in the summer, at least not the way I remembered from home, and the season was marked by the never-ending sound of cicadas—monstrous, screeching creatures I'd assumed to be tiny violinists with delicate legs and antennae, until I saw one dead on the sidewalk, its brown, brittle body like that of a cockroach, the length of my thumb and twice as thick, bulbous eyes and sharp legs, wings alien and frightening, as though it had grown strange and hard with the harshness of this place.

The summer storms returned, thunder and lightning arriving in a swirling instant, the air smelling like metal, copper pennies or blood, animals cowering at the change in electrostatic tension, howling and hissing at the sky, lightning ripping through the clouds, the cicadas briefly silent for they, too, were afraid. The storms shook the house, glass panes shuddering, the chimney rattling on its weight. I spent my time at the window with my husband, inspecting the capricious sky looming beyond our tiny reflections in the glass.

After a storm, trees littered the ground, snapped from sturdy trunks, splintered and sharp. Yet despite the destruction, the leaves were fresh with promise and grasses twinkled with dew, mushrooms already thinking themselves into existence before branches began to rot. Children leapt from front doors, laughing in the aftermath and stomping in puddles, some climbing the fallen trees, shaking water droplets from the boughs.

Herein lies the contradiction of the Plains: they are at once a place of both destruction and renewal, both violence and calm. Often portrayed as simple and idyllic, a flat, empty place in need of filling, their complexity is one that resists definition, even the above binaries. To me, the Plains are neither cruel nor kind. They are indifferent.

◊

When they arrived on the Plains, early homesteaders saw the desolation of the promise they'd traveled across the country to collect—a vast expanse of prairie stretching as far as they could see, no trees let alone houses or humans, even the horizon pulling endlessly away, stretching further from comprehension until it seemed to waver in the distance, sky echoing the isolation.

It is no wonder early settlers on the Plains went mad, found so much horizon and so much sky pressing down unmooring. Some saw waves in the prairie grass, imagined sea in the midst of a dry summer or during the aridity of the Dust Bowl when even the land could not stand the seclusion and threw itself into the air to be carried away on the wind. More than once a man dove from his tractor to the waves he imagined below, the machine cresting over his body, carrying on unconcerned. More than once a man fell into his silo, suffocated in sorghum, drowned by the crop he worried would not find water enough to flourish to harvest.

The predilection to see waves in wheat is not unfounded. The Plains were once home to a Cretaceous sea, with oysters, fish, crocodile, sharks, and large diving birds alive and swimming through the fossil record. More than one farmer, too, dug the bones of sea creatures up from his land, scooping them from the very earth that grew potatoes to feed families who could not imagine the disappeared sea on which they were standing.

Like the weather, the geological history of the Plains is one of contradiction, four glaciation periods leaving the land warm then cool, warm again then cooler still, drought leading to heavy rainfall. Before the ice, when the Laramie Revolution began some 65 million years ago, the Rockies, the Sierra Madres, and the Sierra Nevadas formed, creating immense rain shadows that led to the emergence of grasslands on the central Plains. By the time modern air masses traveling from the Pacific reach the Plains, three different mountain ranges will have disrupted their travel, extracting moisture along the way, making the Plains inhospitable to trees and shrubs—anything but grasses with deep roots. The dry foehn, or chinook winds, that reach the Plains cure the grasses, leaving them dry and brittle for the bison. The winds that reach the Plains are so strong they shape the physical landscape, much like the heavy bison that left marks on stones they encountered during migration, their lifelines carved onto the land.

The Plains as we know them formed when the last Pleistocene glaciers retreated, dried in part by the chinooks and the forests killed by drought. The disappearance of the glaciers must have seemed strange, for the Plains are the result of glaciers breaking the land before the plow, rushing across the surface, smoothing and flattening it to its present state, walls of ice hundreds of feet tall pushing massive boulders thousands of miles, grinding the rocks to fine powder along the way, leaving rich soil tens of feet deep. The glaciers must have swept like waves across the space, the land bracing itself against the inevitable crash.

A Nebraska museum is full of echoes as people walk down corridors lined with the dead bones of history: a giant tortoise shell big as a sledding disc dug up in Kansas; a fierce horned rhino; a long-nailed sloth found in Garden County hunched and big as any man; the monstrous flippers of an ancient Plesiosaur with crocodile head and teeth, its serpent body curling ten feet, discovered right off the highway. Animals of the sea, the forest, and the savannah cohabitate in the exhibits, though they never did in this place. Contradiction, it would seem, is the organizing principle of this curation.

I turn down the hall of natural selection, the most complete record of elephant fossils dug up from each Nebraska county, walking through epochs as Stegodon becomes Mastodon and then the great Mammoth. The smallest bones are as big as my body, tusks shaped like the forklifts construction workers use to remove branches and snow after a storm, our best attempt at survival here modeled after those long extinct.

◊

It was an unusually warm January day, up to 28 degrees from the -6 degree days before, when snow had powdered the prairie like sugar on cakes. Folks ventured outside to milk cows, pull warm eggs from beneath the hens, hitch the horses to head to town for more molasses. Children sat at their desks lined into precision inside sod or wood schoolhouses, chalk dusting their fingertips powdery white.

The cold front came quick, fine snow leaving visibility at zero, the temperature dropping to -20 degrees, -40 in some places. Winds whipped snow heavily across the Plains before folks realized. The Schoolhouse Blizzard of 1888 left thousands caught unaware and killed hundreds, including many schoolchildren trying to find their ways home.

In *The Blizzard Voices,* Ted Kooser writes from the voices of those who survived, deferring to the weather in an attempt to process the human toll, explaining, "When the Alberta Clipper, roaring out of the North, rips apart a straw stack, only the frozen center remains, and each one of these memories is like that center, stripped of digression, picked clean of equivocation. What is left are the core narratives, spare and cold."

It is no coincidence he refers to the center, or core. The Midwest is, after all, called the heartland, occupying the core of the country, pulsing out fire and ice, thrill and rush. This region of the country is called the heartland not only because it rests at the center of the continent, but because like the heart it draws blood to the center before feeding it out to the tributaries through tradition, crops, and the last remaining visions of the idyllic American West.

No matter how much time has passed since sharecroppers were drawn west by promises of land, we remain drawn to the Midwest through agriculture, business, nostalgia. The Plains call us home. Buffalo were drawn to the same spots on the Plains time and again, returning with the seasons as though there were something in their blood memory to tie them to this place, compelling and propelling them back. Sandhill cranes are drawn to and from the Plains as well, returning to the same place for over nine million years, the bones of their dead preserved, the birth of their young ensuring the cycle continues. Pioneers were drawn to the Plains despite the harshness of the weather, despite the way they had to leave their prairie schooners, abandoned hulls like the ribs of great beasts on the prairie. Still, they remained and built towns around what they managed to grow so that now a nation is fed from what comes from this dip in the continent.

Though I had never been to the Midwest before moving there to pursue my PhD, it quickly became home. Living in Nebraska required I listen in order to live well, and in listening to the Plains' moods and mannerisms like I would to an old friend, I grew to know Nebraska in a way I never knew California, though I'd been raised there among the many generations of my family. Over the years, Nebraska sustained me. The fall led to harvest and I gathered my food from farmers I knew rather than a grocery store shelf, taking my lead from animals storing up for the winter and plants settling into stasis to survive the cold. I came to see the winter not as a season to be tolerated, but one of imposed reflection. And its snow and ice made the spring lush, trees budding then bursting to bloom, fields swelling to feed us once more. Even summer with its storms soon seemed a kind of nourishment, providing the water we needed to thrive—especially as California sank ever deeper into drought. When I returned to the place I'd once called home, it seemed drained of vitality, colorless and thirsty and then on fire when dry brush caught and left the state in flames that licked the land right up until the shore.

The inhospitable nature of the Plains with its endless contradiction can draw people in and spit them back out. Kathleen Norris admits in *Dakota: A Spiritual Geography* that "The Plains are not forgiving. Anything that is shallow—the easy optimism of a homesteader; the false hope that denies geography, climate, history; the tree whose roots don't reach ground water—will dry up and blow away." The Plains require grip, require one cling to this place despite hail and strong wind, despite blizzard and drought, require one to dig deep into history, putting down roots. But despite the harsh weather, the way this place does not satisfy the convenient or momentary traveler, there is something here that compels us, demands our awe in the face of its power. There is something about the way this place requires our patience to know it, our forgiveness of its seeming flaws, our appreciation of its indifference. There is something about the way this place does not boast with lavish landscape, the false sense of emptiness that makes us turn inward to examine the ways we live, the ways land shapes our living.

I have found a way to love what is not easy. I like the intimacy required of me here, what I am required to know and learn to make my home. I like that I am humbled, that the Plains remind me land does not exist for my pleasure. That land exists to remind us of our impermanence.

◊

The mythos of the Plains is one of emptiness. Defined by flatness, the Plains are often viewed as lacking depth, but while many wonder where the mountains or the ocean or even the trees are when we look at the Plains, there is much negating the image of vacancy below the surface. More than 75% of prairie grass grows beneath the surface, roots stretching up to twelve feet underground in a tangle of root and bulb. A square meter of sod—big and little bluestem, Indiangrass and switchgrass—can contain twenty-five miles of roots, slender, gnarled, dancing.

Also buried beneath the surface are our human contributions to the Plains: nuclear-missile silos sunk like gopher holes across the prairie. Of the 2,750 land-based nuclear warheads in the United States, approximately 1,850 rest underground on the Plains. It seems as though we've been conditioned to think of the Plains as a harsh place of violent extremes, that we've misinterpreted making a home here with attempting to replicate its power, danger, its showy displays of the potential for destruction.

But our buried weapons are the antithesis of indifference. An attempt at political and global control, they are angry forms of retribution, fire without renewal. Our weapons are modeled after storms: fire cracking the sky into pieces, the air yellow and thick with sulfur, creatures fleeing from the fury.

When I first moved to Nebraska I was afraid of storms, grew sick when tornado sirens wailed and trees shuddered, buildings groaning on their foundations in the wind, electricity gone black as a funnel threatened to wind its way closer. It took time for me to learn to trust this place, to understand that storm was not an act of aggression. Sometimes the funnel wound its way, thankfully, around the basin that sheltered my city. Other cities were not so lucky—a friend spoke of her Joplin home ripped to confetti, the mementos of her childhood scattered as much as a mile away. Over time, the storms made me humble. There was nothing I—nothing we—could do about their awesome power.

Though our weapons are modeled after storms, we have forgotten a critical difference: that storms bring with them renewal. After the winds have ceased, birds return to the trees and green seeps from the sky until it is blue once more. Just before a storm the sky smells sulfurous, but after, the air is as pure as you can find. And while lightning finds its way to the low places, sparking, catching quick and spreading the burn and blaze, the grassland is sustained this way, born and reborn by fire.

Fires kill trees and shrubs, returning their nutrients to the soil. The grasses, whose growth occurs below the surface, are spared. The Plains are meant to withstand flame, for though prairie fires can create temperatures of up to 400 or 500 degrees, these temperatures drop at ground level. Immediately after a prairie fire you can place your palms firmly on sod, for the temperature rarely raises above 65 degrees, protecting seeds and roots and burrowing animals.

We have much to learn about human nature from the Plains—about the ways we are unpredictable, the ways we are beautiful and destructive, restorative and deadly. If nature invites us to be what we are, the Plains invite us to explore our complexities, to live with vigor and fire, with give and take. The Plains ask us to remember that while we live with power and force, we must also remember to be regenerative, restorative. The beach does not exist for our pleasure much as the sky does not exist for our fury.

A life on the prairie is a life unseen, a life underground, something so many of us, with our need for show and appearance, cannot often fathom. While the prairie looks empty to an unaware eye, badgers and ground squirrels, pocket gophers, mice, and moles, move below the surface, each knitting intricate tunnels. Spiraling earthworms and insects stir up nutrients, their lives working with the soil rather than against it, something early settlers could not understand as they fought to contain and maintain unfamiliar crops.

When farmers came to the Plains they couldn't plant because of the roots, didn't know to look underground, to learn the temperament and history of this place. Prairie is fertile and dense, roots spiraling underground, out of our sight and therefore our understanding. Prairie grass roots cling to the soil, firmly entrenched despite soil erosion, able to find water in the most extreme drought. Hardy, unrelenting, their descent below should teach us something about survival and resistance, about working within a system rather than opposed to it, about looking to the past for succor and strength, to understand that what thrives is not simply what is easy.

If we could turn the membrane of the prairie upside-down so what is below rests on top for us to see, the underside of the prairie might look like the cities we build, roads and wires tangling together, our buildings like roots reaching higher and higher towards the sky. While we don't see ourselves in the prairie—historically we have positioned ourselves against it—our very architecture models itself after the Plains.

Settlers eventually learned to make their homes out of sod, some burrowing like the wiser creatures, building into the sides of hills or partly underground, protected from the place by learning to live within it, to become a part of it. Years later we still seek shelter underground, moving to basements and cellars during tornados. When the howling wind comes and the skies splinter, I no longer cower, protected as I am deep in the heart of the land.

SOMETHING FROM NOTHING

The sweetness is a secret, hidden low on branches closest to the ground. If I squat, angling my head beneath bramble, I can find the blackberries no one else noticed. They are full to bursting, juice straining against the skins. They shine purple and glossy in the California heat.

On Sundays, Mama and Daddy and I drive to the berry patch and wander the rows while the sun moves from its position on the horizon to overhead. Heat rises hazy from the bushes like a mirage.

The prickles hurt and my hands stain from crushing berries in unsuccessful attempts to pluck them from the vine. When I look down, I see failure on my fingers.

◊

We do not have money for good fruit. I get apples, the mealy red ones from the bargain bin at the grocery store, and bananas, the kind that are soft and sticky. Mama says that is because they have been kissed by the sun, but I don't want to be loved by someone that leaves a bruise.

On special occasions I get an orange, but it is so rare that the pith worries me and I spend so long trying to pull the fibers from the fruit that the flesh pulps in my hands, leaves them sticky and wanting.

Though we can't afford it, we splurge on good fruit for Daddy. We hide it in a special drawer. I see the shining skins when I clean out the fridge on Saturdays because it—like most of our appliances—is broken. It is my job to use old rags to soak up the leaking cold, wring it into a bucket while my hands prune. I pretend I am Cinderella and I sing to the mice our old cat catches in the dusty fields around our house, then leaves dead on the front porch.

I am not allowed in the drawer, but sometimes I open it to look at the jewels. Soft orange apricots and bright plums, a bag of red cherries. Some of the fruit is waxed and glossy, like the nectarines, but others, like the peaches, are soft and furred. These are the ones I like best, the texture like my new baby sister, like something to love.

When Daddy is happy and his construction team builds a fence despite hundred-degree heat and no one accidentally puts a nail through their thumb, watching it burst like a blueberry, lets me take bites from his fruit.

"Small bites," he says. "Remember."

Apricots are my favorite, tart and tangy on my teeth, and I love to pull the small stone from inside. I ask Daddy if I can keep these pits, evidence of our bounty I plant later in our small backyard, digging in the rocks. Mama laughs, says nothing will grow from that, but I know what she means is that nothing will grow *here*.

We gather at the berry patch early because of the heat, but also to beat the crowds. The parking lot fills quickly with cars full of people visiting from up and down the California coast, coming from San Francisco and Los Angeles to visit the small beach towns and to taste wine, vines full of fruit growing for miles in every direction. City fathers talk on their bulky 90s cellphones while mothers in sundresses take pictures of their children experiencing country life.

We park Daddy's beat-up work truck, chain link and pliers in the bed, in the lot next to sleek cars named after cats. We've escaped our nothing town for the day but I don't feel too bad for standing out since Daddy is the only one who was clever enough to wear boots in these muddy fields.

I worry when I see so many people, worry I will not be able to fill my pail, worry I will only get a few bursts of sweetness on my tongue.

I worry that I am not as clever or quick as the little girls in their matching overalls and straw hats. I wear hand-me-down clothes from my mother—the ones girls at school make fun of—but here it doesn't matter. They already have spots and holes and, now, some sweet berry stains.

I rush down the rows, feverish in my attempt to find and feed myself on the best. If I can gather enough berries and crush them beneath my strong teeth, maybe my smile will stop growing crooked and the kids at school won't call me a vampire.

It is hard, this work, stooping and plucking, and my parents don't have the money to rent the gloves so I prick my fingers and they bleed a bit, mixing with the red berries, a sweet and sour sting I suck onto the tip of my tongue.

"Slow down," Mama says from behind me, where she holds my new sister to her breast. But I know that we have to buy whatever we pick so I go fast, fast. Soon my metal pail is heavy and I drag it on the ground, leaving a trail behind me.

When we pay, my parents wince, but I am so proud.

"Good job," they say anyway.

"We can have berries twice," Daddy cries. "Imagine that!"

I didn't need to worry about the competition. The other children and mothers and fathers give up quickly. They claim a few berries, the ones from the top branches already pecked by the birds, dried out from the sun. They smile for the photos, puckering their mouths after. They leave their pails and buy a few pre-plucked pints from the roadside stand on their ways back home.

🔥

Daddy does not cook often, but when he does it is special. He says so all the time. Daddy's special eggs have lots of seasoning. Daddy's special breakfast rice is full of butter. Daddy is very good, he says, at making something from nothing.

When Mama says there is nothing in the cupboards and I see through the empty shelves to the wall, Daddy says "Let me whip something up," and makes a big show of whistling and singing and pulling the sun-kissed vegetables out of the broken fridge, shaking off the leaking water. He takes the few cans and spices out and tells me that they don't look like they go together but that's why his recipes are so good.

Daddy serves the food up hot, hot so that I can see the steam rise from the plate like a mirage, and he puts it in front of me with a flourish.

The eggs are whipped soft with a salty heat. The rice is sticky and sugar-crusted sweet. Even when I'm hungry for something I see on TV, he can transform a can of vegetables or too-sweet baked beans into the thing I actually wanted to eat.

Daddy looks so eager asking "Isn't that good?" that it always tastes yummy.

There never seems to be enough, but Daddy says what makes his recipes special is that you always want more.

🔥

Sometimes I get greedy, spotting a blackberry not quite ripe, the transformation still underway. I am Mama's best helper, she says— reminds me when my new sister arrives, then the twins a few years later, then two brothers, another sister, so many siblings we can't pick berries anymore—but I can't help but break the rules and claim something for myself.

I pluck the mostly-red berry from the bush and plop it into my mouth where it bursts like the stars I see from my window late at night, when my tummy rumbles after I eat dinner and I lie awake listening to Daddy and Mama whisper about bills across from one another at the empty dining room table.

Shooting stars look like butter smeared across the sky.

But the berries are tart to the point of hurt, making the glands in the back of my throat pulse pain. You cannot make something sweet if it is not.

🔥

Daddy's special recipe for berries is so sweet it makes our teeth ache.

He learned it from his mother, he tells me in the kitchen. Raised in Oklahoma during the Depression, she made something from nothing all the time and it was delicious, he says. He could eat biscuits made of flour and water every day, and he does, telling Mama hers are almost as good.

His mother is dead now from a cantaloupe-sized tumor in her stomach. She died right after I was born, but I see why he liked her cooking so much because when we visit her many sisters and their many children and grandchildren, they make biscuits and gravy and pies and tell us "Eat, eat" while waiting in the kitchen for the men and children to eat first. They like feeding people so much that sometimes there is nothing left for them at all and they wipe the gravy up with their fingers from the plates before they wash the dishes.

We soak the berries to get off the bugs and leaves and dried pollen, and the bodies and bits float to the top of the water like the dead. Mama says to wait until the berries are clean, but we can't help it and we stick our hands in when she isn't looking to sneak a berry. Daddy finds the best ones, dark and heavy, and plops them in my mouth.

"Mmm mmm," he says. "Aren't we lucky?"

When the berries are clean, we pat them dry and Daddy finds a secret can of sweetened condensed milk in our empty cupboards. He hides cans like these for when we need something special.

He puts a handful of berries at the bottom of a bowl, sprinkling them with sugar from the jar he and Mama use to sweeten their coffee. I'm not allowed near the sugar unless I'm cleaning up the ants that trail in the house during summers when it's too hot. I crush their trails on the counter with my fingertips, but Mama and Daddy say don't throw out the sugar.

The sugar glistens on the berries like the snow I've only seen on TV and in my schoolmate's vacation photos. Then comes the best part—Daddy pours the sweet milk over the top, thick like caramel. He stirs it together and we use a big spoon to lap it up.

Daddy and I eat all we could want and our bellies hurt from too much for once. My teeth vibrate and his teeth hurt, dark with coffee and rot, growing grooves between them like the wooden planks he fences for a living.

We pull the berries from the cream with our fingers, lick the sugar off and say, "delicious" like we see in the movies.

When I wash the dishes later, I pretend I'm my grandmother and my aunts. I use my finger to wipe the last of the sugar from the bowl.

�◊

When my parents visit me as an adult—first in Nebraska in my apartment, then later in the Massachusetts apartment and then eventually in the house I share with my husband—I make too much food. Burgers and potato salad and corn and guacamole. Sickly sweet chocolate cakes for dessert.

And I make fruit salad, my favorite. I use strawberries and blackberries, raspberries and blueberries. I use cherries and plums and nectarines and apricots. I add kiwi for color, walnuts for crunch.

My parents go on and on about this salad. They say I didn't need to go to such lengths, that it must have cost so much. I don't tell them I always make this much food, even if it is just my husband and me, that I am forever afraid of running out, of going to bed hungry.

The first time they visit me and my husband on the East Coast, they admire our apartment, staring up at the high ceilings and standing at the large windows that overlook the water. My mother visits occasionally, but the only other time my father has boarded a plane was to come to Nebraska to see me when I graduated with my PhD. Usually I am the one who visits, and when I fly to California, I bring food with me in my suitcase because the cupboards are still empty. I have learned to eat before dinner in case the meal runs out. Now, as my husband and I welcome my parents to our place, I realize this is the first time I've had them to myself, had time alone with my parents and without my many siblings, since those early berry-picking days before my sister was born.

After a lifetime of making something from nothing, my parents are almost out of sugar. Their adult children are hungry, hungry, even after they leave the house. They return home and take food from the cupboards, taking it back to their own hungry families.

My parents are visiting to see if they might retire here one day, because Daddy's skin is dark with age spots like a banana, and at last I understand what it means to be kissed by a lifetime of hard labor in the sun. They need to retire, but don't know how because there is no money, there never was, and they can't imagine quitting work because they can already see through the empty cupboards to the wall.

"Let me whip something special up," I say at breakfast, pouring berries into a pan to make sweet syrup for the pancakes.

The next time they visit, the world will be different. The pandemic will have forced my parents into retirement and they will struggle more than they ever did when I was growing up. My husband and I will have fared better, lucky to have purchased a house on a few acres of woods with room for my parents to maybe live one day if they ever want to call this place home.

The woods will be lush and green, and each spring wild asparagus will shoot up from the ground, raspberries dotting the yard, glistening from the vines.

"Berries growing right in your own yard," Daddy will say. "Imagine that."

FOREST FOR THE TREES

In winter it is easy to think leafless trees look barren. But the forest is full of squirrels, glossy from acorns they've stashed, and the red-bellied woodpecker taps its existence in echoes of both hunger and satiation.

A wild turkey struts the yard. I've named him Gloria, though he doesn't know and clearly does not care much for boundaries of names, of yards, venturing as he does from the woods and wetlands, through the meadow to the lawn to look for worms and crickets. He grows steadily all season, his jet feathers tinged blue in the sun, fanning up as he ages golden and red like a sunset.

He is glorious indeed, which is why I named him for a disco diva who sings about survival. It seems apt for this bird who survives the wilds, who evades the coyotes common here, a pack of five waking me from my sleep by singing on the lawn just earlier this week.

Indeed, a symbol or a song of survival seems fitting for the times.

It is March 2020 and this winter was particularly cruel. All around the world, we are beginning to self-isolate from a virus that has spread steadily since the turn of the new year and decade. We do not yet know what the virus will do—to us, to each other, to our understandings of community and care. We do not yet know that the virus will deepen the divides between regions and generations, will ravage time and memory, will convince some people of their immortality while reminding others of their proximity to death. For now—for once and last—the country, no, the whole world seems connected.

It is hard, however, to be hopeful when our bodies must remain hidden, when we are frozen like the world. To stop the spread, people must stay away from others, must not hug or touch, must avoid those basic contacts we crave especially in the dark and the cold. We, too, are waiting to emerge, to live. The trees look bleak and when I peer into the forest, they tangle, like my heart lately with the cruelty of leaders who do not protect the citizens who voted for them, people beginning to voice that their desires are more important than the safety of those most in need of protection. Time pulses around ache.

But there is movement inside the tree limbs, faint red swellings beneath the bark, the first signs of bloom. It is easy to miss on a single tree, but when I look to the forest I see—over the weeks I wait inside, the forest sends out tender shoots, unfurls blossoms, fills the brightening sky.

I watch the cardinal like a cherry in the wind, the way he endures the harshest of seasons to whistle out for his love. I watch the fox that frequents my yard each morning pounce in the low meadow to pull mice from the desolate field, his arc into the air a crescendo.

This season marks the margin between two borders. When I look close enough, I realize this is the moment of resurrection.

&

In summer I walk in the woods by my house, trails stretching for curving miles along the lake. I pass trees whose bark was stripped away by hungry deer in the lean months. Their trunks are still scarred with survival.

I walk further into the woods and the path splits in two, three, forking forever further. I can no longer hear human noise, only birds on the lake and the wind through the trees. An eastern tiger swallowtail butterfly, bright yellow with black scalloped edging as intricate as lace, leads me, flickering through the shafts of sunlight that make their ways through the branches overhead, stopping to land on lush grasses and purple hepatica, whose blossoms dot the forest floor with the first color of the season. For miles I follow, thankful the butterfly does not frighten like the mottled ducks I startle with the crunch of my footsteps.

At the start of the trail I look down. I pass tiny, empty bottles of cinnamon whiskey and a dozen old condoms, crinkled and translucent like the dried jellyfish of my California coast youth. I look up. I pass old fishing rods by the lake's edge and a child's crude graffiti on a large boulder. Now I do not see a single human, though I know elsewhere folks are heading back to the beach, shopping, gathering in parks, taking advantage of cheap flights despite the warnings to stay home.

I pass a tree gashed by lightning, a scorched hole through the heartwood. Yet still it grows tender leaves, reaching up to the light.

I wonder how old the tree is, how long it has lived despite injury. Forests are some of the longest-living organisms on earth, their growing patterns and practices a primer for survival. Old Tjikko is a 9,550-year-old Norway spruce located in the Fulufjället Mountains in Sweden. Methuselah is a 4,845-year-old Great Basin bristlecone pine growing in the White Mountains of California. The Llangernyw Yew, at least 4,000 years old, grows in a North Wales churchyard.

As I walk, stepping over thick roots that twist up and over my path to weave with the roots of nearby trees, I stop now and then to look at the branches arched overhead. They are careful not to grow into one another in order to leave sunlight for those in the understory. Their reach stops just short of touching, the space between like the iron threads that run between panels of stained glass.

I hold my breath in this forest cathedral.

✿

If you were to gather up a teaspoon of forest soil, it would contain many miles of microscopic fungal filaments, each thinner than a thread. Mycorrhizal fungi send out fine tubes called hyphae through the soil and into the tips of plant roots, creating a dense underground web that has connected trees and plants of various species together into a complex subterranean community for nearly 500 million years.

This mutualistic network allows members of the community to care for one another, transferring resources like water, carbon, nitrogen, defense compounds, and other nutrients and minerals. Trees are attuned to one another's needs—regardless of species—redistributing resources to benefit the community. Strong trees send sugar and phosphorus to trees that are struggling, while older trees with better access to sunlight share with seedlings struggling to survive in the shade.

Trees know they cannot survive alone—they cannot establish the climate and protection they need from the wind and weather, for their inevitable struggle for survival. By creating and protecting a community, however, trees can moderate temperatures, store water, share resources. The network ensures increased establishment success, a higher rate of growth, and the likelihood that the forest will survive unfavorable conditions. It protects both the group and the individual.

The network does not demand lavish praise or recognition. Staring at the rich soil, fragrant with moss and the musk of animals, you would never know what wonders are housed beneath.

Growing up in California, I was familiar with the avocado trees that lined the roads out to the beach. Drivers parked along the grassy shoulder to pluck buttery fruit from the branches and feed themselves on that mellow smoothness.

In Nebraska, I watched storms turned the sky green, sometimes funneled, and in the morning, tree branches peeled away from trunks, the flesh beneath eager and firm, children dancing between the cottonwood boughs, shaking glistening moisture from the leaves.

Now, in Massachusetts, the front fence is more tree than post. This environment encourages growth, and though the old dirt road and the lot were cleared once, trees have already started their ascension.

The fence reminds me of abandoned houses throughout the Midwest from which families fled during the Great Depression, forsaking what they once loved in order to survive. They packed what they could, left the rest—old china, wedding dresses hanging like ghosts in the attic, rocking chairs on the porch. The houses sagged and struggled with the weight, the sense that nothing would ever be the same or safe.

But the trees moved in, worked together to hold up the houses so humanity did not fall.

Standing in the woods, I hear the sound of trees rustling in the wind. It sounds like the swish of fabric, like rubbing fingertips together, like the sea. They sing together, but if I step close to one—the pine in my front yard, the birch lining the forest entryway—I can hear the individual.

Trees hear one another because they listen. Scientists have measured the vibrations thirsty trees send through their trunks, calling on others to send water. Certain trees, like acacia, give off warning gas when they are eaten by animals, signaling to neighboring trees that there is danger.

The other trees listen. They heed the call rather than think themselves removed by location and circumstance. They trust the information and react, pumping their own toxins into their leaves to prepare for the danger, protecting themselves and others.

Despite the dangers of survival—limited resources, different growing conditions, predators, environment, history, happenstance—trees in undisturbed forests do not compete with one another. They synchronize their growth so that all are equally successful. No matter a tree's individual circumstance, the surrounding trees adjust their growth rate to equalize the difference.

Biodiversity stabilizes the forest. The more species there are, the less likely a single species will take over to the detriment of the others.

The sun is out today, though spring rain is forecasted for tomorrow and many days after. I sit outside on my patio and listen to the red-breasted American robins calling to one another about insects in the yard, Eastern phoebes, with their downy grey feathers and dark heads flirting with the breeze. The trees sway back and forth in the wind like a sea kelp forest.

A honeybee flies in front of me, yellow-furred and determined, right into the side of the house. I watch, hoping this setback doesn't agitate the insect into ire, but it simply bounces back and reverses course in the direction from which it came.

It's admirable, this resilience, this flexibility to readjust one's path with hardship, the grace it takes to recognize that what you desire is not always achievable or best.

Here, the snow and the dark return each year, no matter how folks fight or flail against the inevitable. But the trees have learned to drop their leaves, to shift with the seasons, go inward. A forest in winter is a kind of meditation—stillness and calm, clear purpose and gentle breath.

I watch the bee until I cannot see it any longer and all that is left in my view is a tall tree at the edge of the meadow. The tree is one of the oldest on our property, stretching above the others then curving dramatically at the top to towards the lake like an arrow, like a question.

I look at the tree's curve and understand this shift in course as a kindness. The tree did not seek heights unchecked. It did not seek to grow at the expense of others.

It has been one year—now two—that I have isolated in order to protect others and maintain my humanity. Seasons have gone and come back around again and still I am here, with my husband in our home on a few acres of woods, watching and waiting for the world to end.

The woods have been a welcome distraction, a haven that asks only for protection. At least that is how it seems to us these many long months. We've walked many long miles, watched closely as the seasons shifted, as what we thought was dead bloomed back to life. Nature, we've found, calms his manias and soothes my sadness. Staying home, it seems, is the antidote to our marital troubles too. With nothing to do but watch the woods, we've watched too as the stormy winds of our relationship have changed. With nowhere to go, we've come back to each other.

But it is hard to retain the cultural optimism of those early days when I believed the world might unite to do what was right. It is hard now to recognize the real danger, which does not seem to be the virus but a humanity which would rather break than bend.

When I get discouraged, I turn to nature for resilience, for solace. The curved tree at the edge of the yard is tall and old and though gravity and time and many harsh New England winters sought to pull it down and send it crashing over the other trees, sought to make it bend under the pressure of survival, the tree simply leaned in to the hard times, grew up and over them, thriving triumphant.

Now the curved tree sways, waltzing in the wind precisely because of its hardship. I watch and take comfort. The trees around it dance too.

PRACTICING GOODNIGHT

My father exists in darkness.

He wakes before the sun, sits with me and his coffee, leaves before dawn begins to bleed over the horizon. He returns only after the light disappears again in the evening, the sky on fire.

Nighttime is our time. At the dinner table where we eat to fuel our muscles, I sit on Daddy's left, where his heart is, his wallet, his toolbelt full of nails and tape measures and pencils for marking wooden fence planks or my height on the wall. I try to hold quiet and still because Daddy is tired after a long day building the borders that make the world make sense. It doesn't matter what time of day it is, how lonely or scared I am—his fences keep things in place.

I listen while Daddy tells Mama about his day. Daddy's stories take place in sunlight, tales of building along California ocean cliffs and rolling golden hills. He tells a story where he is a hero, but sometimes he shows a wound—a scab where the barbed wire caught him quick or a bloodied finger where the hammer slipped—and I think these stories are too scary.

After dinner Daddy gets strong. I sit with him in the garage and watch him work some more. He builds his muscles now that he is done building fences. He counts to himself and lifts heavy weights and it is dangerous, he says, so I need to hold still and quiet. If I do not listen to Daddy, I could hurt us both.

Through the open garage door, I can see that the stars are out. I can hear the night noises of rabbits and crickets in the dry wheat fields across from our house. They sing with Creedence Clearwater Revival on the radio, but I have rarely seen the rain because it does not storm here, my future with Daddy stretched out golden.

⟡

The blizzard today leaves three feet of snow and an ache in my heart and head, in the joints and marrow that keep me upright. I cannot sleep with the whiteout howling all around. The storm blots out the stars.

All night I try to sleep in my Massachusetts home, but when I wake the world is buried. It is impossible to dig myself free.

⟡

Daddy rarely reads because after work he's too tired for stories. But when he does, he reads to me and together we find the moon.

The book Daddy reads to me is one where a child bunny goes to bed. But the bunny does not want to sleep. He is full of missing. He cannot sleep until he says goodnight—to the clock and the painted cow, to the kittens and mittens. He cannot sleep until he says goodnight to the moon.

The best part is the mouse. He appears on every page, except he's hiding. Daddy pretends he can't find the mouse and I am the clever winner. I am very good at searching—for mice, for bruises and blood Daddy tries to hide, for his dusty work truck at the end of each day rattling back home.

Over and over Daddy and I read a book about a bunny who cannot sleep. At night when he tucks me in, we practice saying goodnight to my toys and trinkets, to the shadows on my wall. Sometimes Daddy opens the curtains and we say goodnight to the moon.

But I do not like to sleep. I am afraid. I am afraid of losing time with Daddy, who is only home a few hours a day. I do not want to miss even a minute. I am afraid of losing Daddy like how his work is dangerous and metal beams can fall or a rattlesnake can strike. At night, in my tiny bed, I am afraid of being alone.

So we practice. We practice saying goodbye, except we call it goodnight. Daddy leaves the room but always comes back. Daddy stands in the doorway until I fall asleep.

My father is near the end of his life. The cancer discovered in his body eight months ago has spread, bled over the horizon so that there seems to be no future where he survives.

His body is weak and he cannot sleep in the hospital because of the noise of tubes and machines, his vitals monitored like a ticking clock.

I live in the future or he lives in the past, and we are always just missing each other. I call my mother from Massachusetts and on the other end of the line California sounds so far away. My father cannot talk, the muscles in his throat atrophied from rigorous chemotherapy, but we have never been much for words. We show our love through what we build, so I try to construct a story where my father lives. I try to write a world where his borders never fall, where wood does not rot from rain or termites, where fences and fathers mean forever.

I look backward to my home on the West Coast from my place on the East Coast. When my father still sees the sun, I am already looking at the moon.

We wake before the sun. The living room is cold because running the heat is expensive, but in the mornings Daddy turns it on just for us. I can smell dust burning as the heater groans to life, and the smell of Daddy's soap and the sawdust that never leaves his skin, sweet cedar lingering in his knuckles and long curls.

I am brave in Daddy's hug, his arms wrapped around me so that his muscles are my muscles even though I sometimes leave my spinach and meat on my plate and he says I won't get strong. I'm supposed to sleep for strength too, but this is hard on the nights I have to be alone.

I cannot sleep with the sound of the wind or the clock ticking or even my beating heart. I sneak out of my covers so often Daddy makes me a little bed on the floor of my parents' room. At first I try to stay awake, to be with Daddy just a little longer before the night is gone and so is he. But eventually I am warm and safe and drift off listening to my parents whisper.

Mornings so early they might as well still be night, I sneak with Daddy to the living room. We warm by the heater and then we stand together silent at the sliding glass door to watch the stars fall, to watch the sun rise.

"Good morning, moon," Daddy says and we laugh because it is funny to outsmart time, to live between night and day.

It is dark when my father first arrives at my home in Massachusetts. We have not seen each other in nearly two years because the pandemic put our lives on pause. We have both aged since we last saw each other. I weep like a girl in the airport.

I run into his arms and the hypervigilant fear I have carried with me melts because we are together. After so many years apart, we are greedy with togetherness.

My parents have missed the lunar eclipse by a few weeks, but the waxing moon still leaves little light when we arrive in the woods. My father is exhausted—this is the moment I realize something is not right—but he jumps from the car to inspect the property. Over the long visit, we will walk the perimeter a dozen times, will wander through the woods to the water, will read local real estate listings and property charts and building plans like treasure maps.

Throughout the visit, the moon grows until it is bright and full and we stay up late listening to the sound of night noises. I fret over my father, who seems ill though he insists he is fine like he did when I was a child and he shielded me from his many hurts. Mornings we stand by the sliding glass door watching the sun, our reflections staring back at us in the glass, and my father says how proud he is that I have built such a wonderful life, such a wonderful home.

I cry when he leaves—on Father's Day—because I always cry at endings. The day he arrives back in California, he goes to the doctor at my insistence and receives the cancer diagnosis.

Now when I wake in the night, I exist, for a moment, between dreams and reality. It is welcome, this unknowing, this numb.

But then I reach for water or make my way to the restroom or turn to adjust my pillow. And it is there—the realization that my father is ill.

Since his diagnosis I have seen many moons wax and wane like my grief, which is also pulled by the tides. Sometimes it seems I might drown. I have tried to accept the inevitability of his death—numbers and figures the way my father taught me to solve problems, to build solutions. But I have failed to build a fence around my heart. All the walls I try to build come crumbling down each time the cancer spreads to another lymph, another organ, each time a new shadow reveals itself on the CT scan, my father's body lit up celestial.

I could not sleep so doctors prescribed drugs to dull me into dreamlessness. I could not close my eyes, afraid my father would be gone when I woke, so now I take pills to turn off my head and heart. My sleep is heavy. On the rare occasion a dream seeps through the haze, my father is young and strong, speaking to me across time, both of us living between past and present.

Only in sleep do I forget his illness. Only in sleep can I escape the ticking countdown to his end. Depending on the day of the month, I can either see the glow of the moon or I am shrouded in darkness.

Each time I remember, my stomach drops and I am breathless, sinking like a ship caught at sea in a storm, like a fence taken down by the wind.

This happens a few times each night, the shock of my father's diagnosis. Each time I wake, he is dying all over again.

⟡

In *Goodnight Moon*, the bunny is afraid of being left alone. The large room is a gulf between him and his parent. The room is lit, but outside it is dark and he worries what will happen if the lights go out.

Published in 1947 as an antidote to the trauma of world war, the book promises that sleep is not a danger. It promises that no matter what happens, we can relax into dreams and that when we wake, everything will be as it was. There is safety in sameness: the kittens will always be frolicking, there will always be a comb and brush, a bowl of mush. And there, in a chair, a watchful parent. Always.

◊

Soft foam bounces beneath my feet, my body buoyant despite the heavy spacesuit. The moon room of the children's museum glows with neon stars that illuminate the matte black emptiness of the small enclosure. I crouch to get inside, but Daddy cannot fit so I am all alone, surrounded by the cosmos. I am amazed and afraid there in the dark as I stare back down to Earth.

The tiny marble painted on the wall and, later, the images inside the spaceship make Earth seem mesmerizing. But the edges of the continents do not look the same as they do on maps, and no matter how I try, I cannot locate home. I do not know where one thing ends and another begins, do not know what part of the planet sees the sun and what part sees the moon. If Daddy is in the part that cannot see the moon, then how will he see me waving, how will he know if I am happy or hurting?

I feel frantic. Daddy rarely gets time away from work so today is special, but still I feel the weight of gravity pulling me to the realization that one day I will not be able to get back to him, that one day the darkness of space will close all around and I will not be able to find my way home, and that even if I do, the time and space it takes me to get back might be too much, everything different by the time I land.

When I crawl back to find Daddy waiting for me at the entrance, he asks, "How was the moon?" and I pretend myself brave. I wrap my arms around his legs, stand on his heavy work boots for support. And he must know the moon is no place for me because he doesn't ask me any more questions about that cold dead rock.

Instead, we go to another exhibit. We stand together tight as a hug inside a hula-hoop. We pull a string to lift it up and around and over us, until we are left surrounded by a glittering soap bubble. We hold still. We hold our breath. We try not to let it burst.

◊

My father is waning. Even before the cancer, his body was exhausted from a lifetime of manual labor. After he retired, my father began to sleep longer in the mornings, rising sometimes after the sun. Prior to his illness, he seemed a different man when I visited throughout my twenties and into my thirties. Accustomed to different time zones, I woke well before he did and sat whispering with my mother over tea in the dark.

But when he rose, I saw him rested. My father was nearly un-recognizable without pain and strain on his face, marking his steps. He did not limp or move stiffly, did not suffer a hernia or a slipped disc or broken finger or any of the other hundred hurts he'd ignored throughout my childhood in order to give me the stars.

Now my father danced down the stairs and flung open the win-dows to greet the day by saying "Good morning, morning." He sang while he made me breakfast, no matter how long I'd already been awake, performing his show of pulling secret cans of something spe-cial out of the cupboards. We sat for long hours talking.

Before the pandemic, when I made the trip home to California from Massachusetts, we wandered the dusty fields examining all the fences he'd built throughout the decades, the whole region mapped by his work. We searched the coastal tidepools and gathered starfish and moonstones from the beach, galaxies in our hands.

Midday my father would sleep again. He would retire to bed and close the curtains and drift into a welcome slumber. It reminded me of my own childhood, when my parents insisted I nap long after most of my peers because I could never sleep through the night, because I insisted on rising so early, keeping myself awake, calling for my father to light up the night.

When I napped, I would fall into a fitful slumber, feverish and fran-tic. I would dream strange bursts of color and chaos and stir from sleep red-faced and damp, jolting into consciousness afraid I had missed something, that I was waking to a strange and terrible new world.

Now I am restless while my father rests. I am the same age he was those many years ago when he spent long hours away and I saw him only in darkness. I live as far away from my father as the country al-lows. If you gazed on our continent from space you could not capture us both at once.

Overhead, the mock sky domes with stars, constellations easily etched for an elementary class to identify. The parachute planetarium smells like rubber and I can hear the sound of the projector, the rustle of bodies against the sides of the half globe we've crawled inside. Above us is Orion's belt, which reminds me of Daddy's—heavy with tools for fixing things like broken bikes or busted feelings when I misspelled "jewelry" in the spelling bee.

My favorite constellations are the Big Dipper and Little Dipper: Daddy and me. I like how my constellation fits inside his, just like our hands. I search the sky for us every time I look up just like how I search for the mouse in my bedtime book. We are always there, our star bodies an anchor to orient me when I am at sea, when nothing seems to make sense.

◊

My father exists in darkness.

Nothing from my childhood remains except the moon and the stars, and even these will burn out one day. In the meantime, California is always on fire and each year more of the ocean cliffs simply give up and slide into the sea. There is little life left in the tidepools. The world I woke to as a little girl, that I bid goodnight to with my father by my side, has washed away and all that remains are my footprints in the sand, those too threatening to vanish.

The cancer continues to spread. I can't visit as often as I'd like because the roles have reversed and now I work long hours while my father waits for me to come back home. My father finally has time to read, during his six-hour chemotherapy infusions and all the recovery time that follows his many surgeries, but he is too tired for stories. Soon he cannot even eat to feed his muscles. Doctors insert a feeding tube, giving him liquids through an IV. For the first time I am bigger than my father, but I do not know how to be strong.

I try. I help him walk until he cannot. I call every doctor. I send packages to show I care.

My father is exhausted, so when I visit—until the pandemic surges again like the tides and my grief and it is too dangerous for him if I return—I sit beside him for long hours in exchange for silence. And then I fly back to Massachusetts like a space traveler. From high above the clouds, the world looks tidy, orderly with edges and borders clearly marked. I close the window, though, because it hurts too much to look at the sun, then the moon, those glowing celestial bodies. The airship hurtles me through space, through time until I land in a different day.

I am still a child. I am still searching for a mouse, a moon, for anything that will keep me with Daddy longer. I do not want to close my eyes and wake up to a different world. I am still so afraid of the dark.

All these years later I still cannot sleep. I do not want to say goodnight when it means goodbye.

ACKNOWLEDGEMENTS

Endless gratitude to the journals where these essays first appeared: *Bellingham Review*, *Crab Orchard Review*, *Fourth Genre*, *New England Review*, *Pithead Chapel*, *Southeast Review*, *Sycamore Review*, and *Zone 3*. I am grateful, as well, to *Best American Essays* for listing several of these essays as Notable.

Thanks to the Split/Lip Press team for making space for this book about searching for place. To Kristine Langley Mahler, for your commitment to work that is lyric and strange. To Lauren Westerfield for the close collaborative editing that helps a writer and book discover who and what they were trying to be all along. To David Wojciechowski for designing a cover that puts into pictures the memories in my mind. And to the entire team for their support of this nostalgic collection.

To the communities of writers, faculty, and students I've had the privilege of working with at California State University-Fresno, University of Nebraska-Lincoln, and Bridgewater State University. You inspired the stories in this collection and shaped my very ability to tell them. I'm eternally grateful for conversations about life and writing with Halina Adams, Annie Bierman, Ilana Masad, Bruce Owens Grimm, and SJ Sindu. And finally, a good playlist, like a good friendship, is hard to find, and I am indebted to Daniel Froid and Mitch Hobza for providing both through many years and many homes.

To Brady Reynolds, who has felt like home for much of my life, and has traversed the country with me in search of stories. You make me whole when the world is falling apart. Even when I am restless, I always come back to you.

To Barbara and Chuck Wilbur, friends and adopted grandparents who taught me what it means to love someone for all of your life.

To my mother, whose endless love follows me no matter where I live. Despite how much time passes, your lap still comforts me like I am a child.

Finally, to my father, who taught me how to dig deep in order to build worlds. Missing you is a story I am still trying to tell.

SARAH FAWN MONTGOMERY is the author of *Quite Mad: An American Pharma Memoir* (The Ohio State University Press, 2018) and three poetry chapbooks. She is an Assistant Professor at Bridgewater State University.

Made in United States
Orlando, FL
10 January 2023